Designs for Teddy Bears

MILNER CRAFT SERIES

Jenny Bradford's Designs for Teddy Bears

SALLY MILNER PUBLISHING

First published in 1996 by
Sally Milner Publishing Pty Ltd
RMB 54 Burra Road
Burra Creek
NSW 2620

Reprinted 1997

© Jenny and Don Bradford, 1996

Photography by Ben Wrigley
Styling by Sarah Houseman
Printed in Hong Kong

National Library of Australia
Cataloguing-in-Publication data:

Bradford, Jenny, 1936 -
Jenny Bradford's design for teddy bears.

ISBN 1 86351 197 0

1. Teddy bears. 2. Handicraft. 3. Soft toy making. I.
Title. II. Title: Designs for teddy bears. (Series:
Milner craft series).

745.5924

ACKNOWLEDGEMENTS

Sincere thanks to the following people who have helped me with projects for this book: Molly Bouquet for the delightful crocheted outfit featured in the Teddy Togs chapter; Elizabeth Halfnights for checking Don's cross-stitch graphs and working the tennis bear picture; Jean Townsend for her lovely fabric art applique; Peter Trainor, owner of Teddy & Friends in Canberra, for his support and the loan of bears and furniture for photography; Raewyn Bastion for the delightful stick pin pictured on the jewellery pillow; and to Julie Hanks for the supply of Gumnut Yarns. I am indebted to Dee Glossop of Dee Glossop Teddy Bears and Accessories, Adele Rowe of Serendipity Collection and Gerry Warlow of Gerry's Teddy and Craft Designs for their constant help, encouragement and advice. Together with many talented bear artists, they are doing a great deal to place Australian teddy bears at the forefront of the bear world.

Producing a book is a team effort and I am lucky to have a very talented group of people supporting me on this publication. My publisher Sally Milner, photographer Ben Wrigley, designer Sarah Housman and editor Kathryn Lamberton, have all enhanced my work with their expertise. Last but not least my husband, Don, who has, as always, made an enormous contribution to the final work including designing the cross-stitch patterns and working most of them for photography. (In fact if I'm not careful I might find myself out of a job!)

Jenny Bradford, 1996

CONTENTS

DEDICATION

In fond memory of my dear friend and fellow teddy bear enthusiast Pat Lovelock (1929-1995).

A weekend spent manning adjacent stands at a show in Melbourne in 1988 was more than sufficient time for Pat to infect me with her enthusiasm and love for teddy bears. Pat generously shared her knowledge and expertise with many of us and in so doing will continue to influence our work and ideas long after her untimely death.

George, one of the most treasured bears in my collection, was made by Pat in 1988. It is pictured in the colour section of this book.

INTRODUCTION

Teddy bears are quite remarkable: they have no language barriers, no age barriers, and as a result I am sure they must be one of the most loved inanimate beings in the world. They can be collectors' items with huge price tags or cost but a few dollars and become lifelong companions.

For those who create them they are far from inanimate objects. In fact they exhibit many human characteristics which is probably why so many find the art of bear making so fascinating.

Like people, no two bears are ever alike. Even mass-produced factory-made bears differ because the position of the ears, eyes, nose and the line of the mouth will vary just a little from bear to bear. If you use the same basic pattern and make it up in different types of fabric, your bears will still not look related.

All the bears created for this book are made from three basic patterns. Alternative leg and muzzle patterns for Scallywag further increase the possibility of varying your creations. If you have never made a bear before, the first chapter will help to simplify this enjoyable task.

For those who love bears or have family and friends who love bears, I have included in this book many items suitable for gifts. There are items for baby, including a practical carry bag for baby's needs, bear bibs and applique designs suitable for cot blankets. And there are teddy bear clothes for the little ones who like dressing and undressing their favourite bear and applique and cross-stitch designs for small children who like to wear bears.

Adult bear lovers have not been forgotten. Patterns for practical carry bags, quick and easy fabric applique for garments and gifts, embroidery designs for pictures and pillows, and tiny bear brooches have all been included.

CHAPTER 1

MAKING A TEDDY BEAR

Creating a teddy bear is always a challenge whether it is the first one ever or one of many. The challenge for most of us is to create a bear that has character and personality. It may turn out to be happy or sad, young or old, boy or girl, fat or skinny, firm and rigid or soft and cuddly. Countless different bears can be made from a basic pattern simply by changing the material and finishing details.

CHOOSING YOUR PATTERN

The number of patterns available is endless and there is also enormous variety in shape and size. Patterns designed for fur fabric bears make an allowance for the pile on the fabric and a good pattern will detail the length of pile ideally suited to the size of the bear. This does not mean that you cannot experiment with different fabrics but it is important to be aware that you will create a very different bear. In general, patterns designed for fur fabric bears do not work in plain fabric such as homespun, calico or velvet; the bear will look very lean or skinny. Likewise, in reverse, a plain fabric pattern is generally not suitable for making a fur fabric bear.

FABRIC

There are literally hundreds of fabrics available for bear making so choosing a fabric can be a little confusing. Prices range from $30 per metre for synthetic fabric to over $150 a metre for top-of-the range English and German mohair. Most of these fabrics are between 140cm (55") and 150 cm (60") wide. Fabrics can often be purchased from suppliers in economical sizes such as 'fat quarters', 50 cm (20") by half the width of the fabric. If you intend making a number of bears in the same fabric, it is usually more prudent to buy a larger piece of fabric than a number of smaller pieces.

Synthetic fur

This comes in a variety of pile lengths, with two different types of backing fabric. *Woven back* synthetic has a firm backing and will not stretch and give during the stuffing process; *knit back* synthetic has a certain amount of stretch which can affect the finished proportions of the bear.

Synthetic furs feel wonderfully soft and they are washable which makes them the best choice for a young child's bear. The modern-style, softly stuffed cuddly bears are generally made of synthetic fur. However, the very thick plush pile is sometimes more difficult to sew than mohair fabric.

Mohair fur

This fabric has been the traditional choice for bear making since the early 1900s. It is made from Angora goat fur and has a strongly woven cotton backing which is easy to sew both by hand and machine. The fur is less dense than synthetic fur and therefore the seams are less bulky.

Mohair comes in many different pile lengths and colours, and it can be hand dyed for individual effect. Types of pile also vary from plain, straight pile to swirly, wavy, string, distressed and sparse, to name but a few!

OTHER FABRICS

There are other types of fabric, such as alpaca and merino wool, available from some stockists. A fabric known as 'Craft Fur' can be an inexpensive substitute. 'Craft Fur' is a felt-like synthetic fabric, with a fluffy finish, which is washable and easy to use. (The white bear in the lower left corner of the cover picture is made from 'Craft Fur'.)

Miniature bear fabrics

It is important when selecting fabric for tiny bears to choose one that has a firm backing that will not fray. This makes construction easier. There are some very short pile mohair fabrics but the easiest to handle are the plush mini-bear fabrics available from teddy bear supply stockists (see page 95).

As with many forms of creative work, generally it is advisable to use the best materials that you can afford. The amount of time spent on a project may be the same, but your satisfaction will be greatly reduced if the result is below expectation and construction has proved difficult owing to an inappropriate choice of fabric. My advice is to shop with bear supply specialists where you will receive help and advice, particularly if you are inexperienced.

JOINTS

Plastic, cotter pin, locknut joints

Plastic joints are available from most craft shops and are the best choice for children's bears which usually require frequent washing. Traditionally, however, bears were jointed with locknut joints or cotter pin (split pin) joints. Most artist bear makers agree that, for larger bears, locknut joints are more secure and less likely to work loose than cotter pin joints, and they also add a little weight to the bear.

Cotter pin joints are usually used for miniature bears. Small fine cotter pins are easy to turn with fine-nosed pliers whereas the larger cotter pins needed for larger joints require a strong wrist to turn them satisfactorily.

Locknut joints are held in place with a small spanner and the bolt is tightened with a second spanner or a screwdriver, depending on the type of bolt used. I find hexagonal-headed bolts easier to use, but it is a matter of personal preference. Head joints require a plain nut instead of a locknut and, once tightened, this should be fixed in place with a spot of super glue to prevent it working loose over time.

Craftwood discs, with metal washers, are used on each joint. Discs used with bolts have a larger centre hole than those used with cotter pins. The metal washers are used to prevent the bolts or cotter pins wearing away the disc. Some bear makers use a felt disc between the wood disc and the fur fabric to prevent wear on the fur. Cotter pins sometimes have slender heads which can pull through the discs. To prevent this occurring, open the pin and thread a 6 mm (¼") washer onto the pin and close it again before inserting in the joint.

Joints are assembled as detailed below

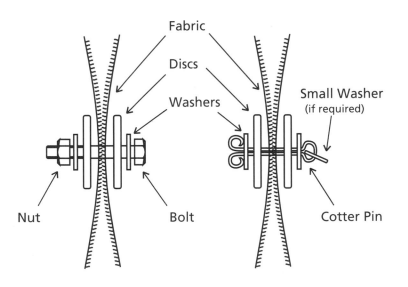

String joints

Following are instructions for attaching arms and legs with beads, as for Tiny:

1. Cut a strong thread about 50 cm (20") long, fold in half and thread the two cut ends through the eye of a doll needle.

2. Pass the needle through the body at the base of the dart, then pass the needle through one arm from the inside to the outside. Thread a bead onto the needle and return the needle through the arm and body to approximately 2 mm (1/16") from the starting point. Check carefully that the threads run freely before you pull the needle through the second time. It is essential that you do not pierce the threads with the needle at any time.

3. Pass the needle through the loop of thread and test to make sure that the thread will tighten when you pull on the cut ends. Remove the needle and leave the ends hanging.

4. Repeat the process on the other side of the body to attach the opposite arm. Vary the needle position slightly so that you do not pierce any of the threads already in position. Test both threads as before.

5. Pull firmly on the cut ends of the threads from one side and pass the needle through just behind one arm and out at the top of the body where the threads will be covered when the head is positioned.

6. Repeat with the threads from the opposite arm, then tie them very firmly and cut off.

7. Joint the legs as for miniature bears, using beads.

String jointing for miniature bears

1. Thread a doll needle with a strong thread, doubled. Leaving a long tail hanging, pass the needle through the body, then through one limb from the inside to the outside.

2. Pass the needle back through the limb and the body, using a slightly different needle position so that the original thread is not entangled.

3. Thread on the second limb and pass the needle back to the starting position.

4. Tie the thread ends together very firmly, pulling the limbs firmly against the body, and trim the ends.

STUFFING

There are many different types of stuffing that you can use. For beginners, good quality polyester filling is the cheapest and the easiest to handle. For those who prefer natural fibres, ginned cotton or wool fleece products are an alternative.

The inclusion of plastic pellets in the filling will result in a softer feel and a more poseable bear. Using lead pellet filling in miniature bears is somewhat controversial and opinions vary as to the health safety risk. To my mind, bears treated as collectors' items pose no problems, and lead pellet filling does add weight and balance - and character - to the bear. But this type of filling should not be used for bears that will be handled frequently or played with by children in unsupervised situations. Care should be taken when working with pellets to minimise handling by wearing gloves or using a tiny spoon or funnel to insert the filling. Make sure also that any spillages can be contained.

CLIPPING THE FUR

This requires a lot of courage if you are new to bear making but it is an essential part of creating a bear. Normally done after stuffing, it is used to sculpture the face. The dilemma is how much and where? Usually the muzzle, and sometimes the eye area, is involved. The pattern for Scallywag includes a separate muzzle section designed to make this process a little easier; in fact, for this pattern, it is safe to clip the muzzle piece before assembly so that if the scissors slip the piece can be re-cut.

Some trim the muzzle fur back to the backing fabric, which is often easier than going half way, but this will result in a bear with a slender muzzle.

Practise on a scrap of fabric. Brush the fur against the grain to make it stand up, then clip with sharp fine-pointed scissors, taking off just the tips of the fur all over the required area. Repeat until the pile length has been reduced by the required amount.

STITCHING

There is always a certain amount of hand stitching in bear making. Some of us do more than others and hand stitch from start to finish. Whatever your preference, careful attention to detail will improve the finished result.

1. Match the pieces as instructed and whip the edges together by hand (see page 94), pushing the fur away from the cut edges as you work. These stitches are sewn with ordinary thread and should remain within the seam allowance but do not have to be neat or particularly close.

2. Sew along seam lines by machine using ordinary thread, or by hand using a small neat back stitch in a strong thread (e.g. Gütermann top stitch thread). Pull the stitches firmly as you work them.

3. Uneven seam lines will show up on the foot pads of the bear and for this reason I recommend sewing them by hand on all bears.

4. Ladder stitch (see page 92) is used to close all openings after stuffing. Use strong thread and small stitches.

EYES

Traditionally, bears mostly had boot button eyes. These are now hard to find and are greatly prized by many bear artists. Glass eyes are now a popular choice and are inserted after stuffing, as follows:

1. Using sharp scissors, an awl or stiletto, make a small hole in the fabric and stuffing.

2. Thread the eye onto a long length of strong thread, doubled.

3. Thread a long doll needle with both ends of the doubled thread and pass the needle down through the hole and out at the base of the head, close to the edge of the joint disc.

4. Repeat for the other eye, bringing the needle out close to the first threads. A small dot of glue behind each eye can be used for added strength.

5. Pull the threads firmly to indent the eye and tie off securely. Pass the ends through the fabric and tie a second time to strengthen.

Safety snap-lock eyes are safer for children's bears. These have to be put in before stuffing the head so they cannot be adjusted after stuffing and can be rather prominent unless stitching is used to indent them.

NOSE

There are many different styles of nose used on bears and this is one of the features that will individualise your bear.

Noses are generally worked in stranded cotton, Coton Perle 5 or 8 embroidery threads, the thickness of the thread being chosen according to the size of the bear and your own preference. To provide a smooth surface to work on, it is essential to clip back the fur to the backing fabric so that it does not work through the stitching. A certain amount of padding will generally improve the look of the nose.

I prefer the following method, probably because I am an embroiderer and it works well for the smaller bears I generally make.

1. Outline the nose size with straight stitches.

2. Fill in the area with straight stitches, closely worked in the opposite direction to the final stitching.

3. Work the final row of stitching, starting with a stitch directly down the centre line. Work away from this centre stitch, laying alternate stitches on each side of the centre line. This will help to keep the nose symmetrical.

For large bears the following method can be used.

1. Cut a felt shape and position with a tiny spot of glue.

2. Work the embroidery stitches over the shape, starting with a stitch down the centre line and working from side to side. Providing the original shape is symmetrical, you should not have any problem with the symmetry of the finished nose.

MOUTH

The mouth is generally worked in straight stitch or fly stitch (see page 92). Positioning and angle will vary the bear's expression. Upturned corners depict a smile, downward-angled stitches a solemn expression. The outer corners of the mouth are often placed approximately in line with the eyes.

USEFUL TOOLS AND EQUIPMENT (see colour plate 2)

- template plastic for making pattern templates
- cotter pin turners for joints
- super glue to seal head joint nuts
- small spanners and pliers for tightening joints
- forceps or flat nose pliers for pulling needles through tough places and turning small bears
- long doll needles for attaching eyes and string jointing
- stuffing sticks, chopsticks or small screwdriver for packing down stuffing
- small sharp scissors for cutting out and clipping fur
- small wire brush for grooming
- stiletto or awl for making holes in fabric for eyes and joints
- Fray-check can be used to prevent fraying and stretching of seam allowances. (Beware! Apply sparsely, otherwise it will make the seam allowance very stiff and difficult to work.)

DOS AND DON'TS OF BEAR MAKING

- Do make templates of the pattern and draw the pattern onto the fur backing ready for cutting. Don't pin a paper pattern to fur fabric as this will not give you an accurate result.
- Do whip stitch pieces together (see page 94) and push the fur away from the cut edge. This will make stitching easier and more accurate and will save time later because the fur will not get trapped in the seams and have to be eased out.
- Do make sure that the joints are properly tightened. They will loosen up after the bear has been stuffed, especially if it has been stuffed very firmly, and when the bear is handled.
- Do take care with stuffing; shape and mould the parts as you go. Heads are generally stuffed very firmly; bodies and limbs are stuffed according to preference and the style of the bear. Make sure the stuffing is packed firmly into areas such as the nose, hands, feet and the covering of joints. Use good quality stuffing that does not 'ball' - and take your time.
- Do use small fine-pointed scissors for cutting out the fur

and cut against the direction of the pile, sliding the scissors under the pile and cutting the backing fabric only. Don't use large scissors and don't chop the pile, otherwise the seams will show on the finished bear.

- Do experiment with eye, ear and nose positions before completing the head. Ears can be held in place with pins, and different-shaped noses can be cut from felt and pinned in place for consideration. You can embroider over the felt if you want a more prominent nose. Use pins to hold the mouth thread in place to help you decide on the final placement. Eyes are crucial when it comes to expression. Size makes a huge difference. Large, widely positioned eyes will give a younger look and a softer expression. Small, closely positioned eyes will give a totally different character to the same bear. Experiment, using felt circles pinned into position.

- Do pay attention to final finishing. Brush the fur and loosen any fur trapped in the seam line with a needle.

- Don't forget to tag your bear with a swing tag detailing the fur type, filling, etc. You can also sew a signed label into a seam or sign one of the foot pads. Attractive labels can be made by writing on a piece of ultra suede with a fabric pen.

CHAPTER 2

SCALLYWAG

A 25 cm (10") bear; 18 cm (7") when sitting
Colour plate 1

T here are six versions of this bear in the front cover picture, all created in different suitable fabrics, from very short pile synthetic to mohair with a 1.6 cm (⅝") pile length. The fabrics used for these bears were:

BEAR	MATERIAL
Centre row, far left and right	German mohair, 1.3 cm (½") pile
Centre row, second from left	German mohair, swirly 1.6cm (⅝") pile
Centre row, second from right	German woven back synthetic, short pile
Bottom row, far left	'Craft Fur', synthetic felt-type fabric
Bottom row, second from left	German mohair, 1 cm (⅜") pile.

REQUIREMENTS

- *1 'fat quarter' of mohair fur fabric, 50 cm x 70 cm (20" x 27 ½") (makes 2 bears)*
- *1 set of joints with 25 mm (1") discs for the head and 20mm (¾") discs for the limbs*
- *1 pair of 7 or 8 mm glass eyes*
- *7.5 cm (3") square of felt or suede for the paws*
- *Coton Perle 8 or stranded cotton for the nose and mouth*
- *Strong thread for sewing*
- *Stuffing of your choice*

INSTRUCTIONS - PATTERN

Before you start, read all the general instructions in Chapter 1 and note that all seam allowances are 3.5 mm (approx. ³⁄₁₆").

1. Position the templates, as shown in the layout diagram, and draw around them using a fine line marker or pencil. Note: Take care to reverse the pattern pieces when required (as shown in the layout diagram) and ensure that the pile of the fabric runs in the direction indicated by the arrows on the patterns.

2. Cut out carefully and Fray-check edges if desired.

Scallywag

Layout of fur parts with alternative leg shapes

Scallywag-50cm x 25cm

Large size-50cm x 46.5cm

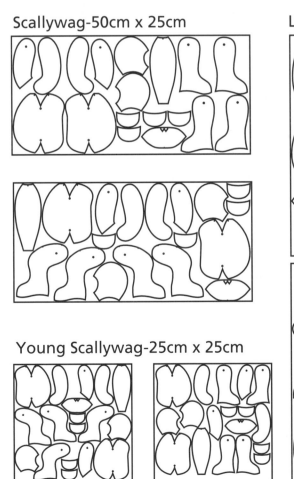

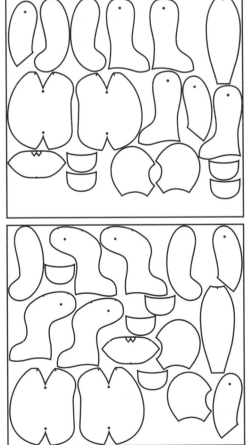

Young Scallywag-25cm x 25cm

INSTRUCTIONS - HEAD

1. Join head gusset to the side head pieces A-B.

2. With point C matching on the muzzle and centre gusset pieces, join seam D-C-D.
   Note: If using the alternative muzzle pattern for a bear with a longer, more pronounced muzzle, stitch the two small darts before matching the centre point C on the head gusset and joining points D-C-D.

3. Fold muzzle in half and sew from I through D to E.

4. Turn head.

5. Using strong thread doubled, run a row of gathering stitches around the neck edge.
   Note: Ensure that the thread ends are long enough so that you can hold them firmly to pull up around the neck joint after stuffing.

6. Stuff the head firmly, insert the neck joint, pull up the gathering thread and tie off securely.

7. Sew on the ears and position the eyes (see page 18) at the point where the gusset seams join the muzzle.

8. Embroider the nose and mouth using a single strand of Perle 8 or two strands of stranded cotton (see page 16).

INSTRUCTIONS - BODY

1. Sew the side darts in the two body pieces.

2. Sew the centre front and back seams, breaking the stitching at the neck joint to allow the head joint to pass through.

3. Turn the body.

4. Joint the head to the body (see page 11).

INSTRUCTIONS - LIMBS

1. Sew the leg seams, then insert the foot pads. Turn.

2. Sew the paw pads to the inner arms, then sew the arms. Turn.

Scallywag

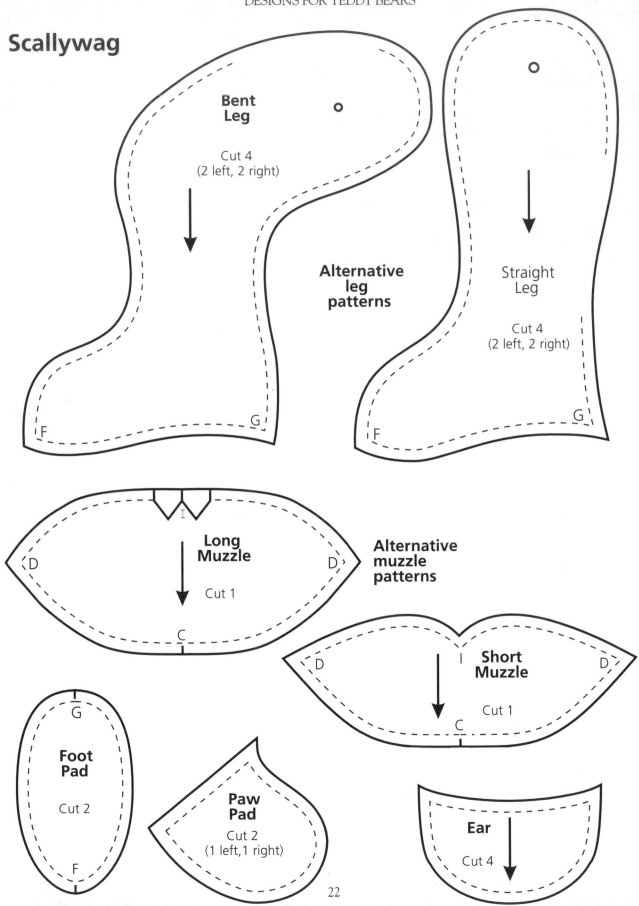

Bent Leg

Cut 4
(2 left, 2 right)

Alternative leg patterns

Straight Leg

Cut 4
(2 left, 2 right)

F   G

F   G

Long Muzzle

Cut 1

D   D

I

C

Alternative muzzle patterns

Short Muzzle

Cut 1

D   D

I

C

Foot Pad

Cut 2

G

F

Paw Pad

Cut 2
(1 left, 1 right)

Ear

Cut 4

22

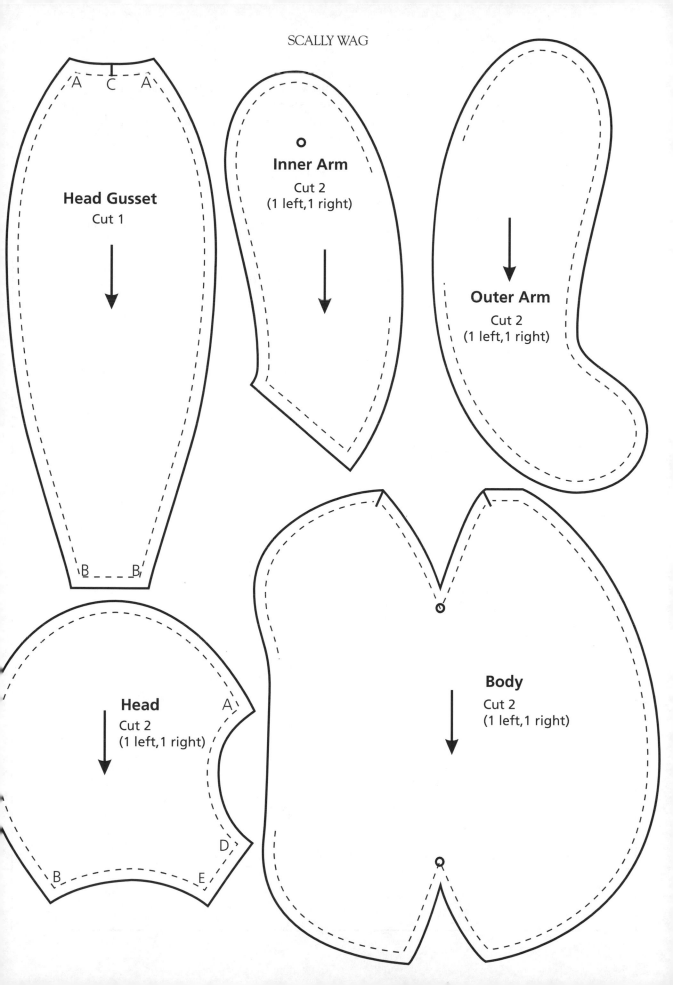

Head Gusset
Cut 1

Inner Arm
Cut 2
(1 left, 1 right)

Outer Arm
Cut 2
(1 left, 1 right)

Head
Cut 2
(1 left, 1 right)

Body
Cut 2
(1 left, 1 right)

3. Joint the arms and legs to the body, inserting the joints into the limbs first and then through to the body (see page 11). The small circles on the patterns indicate the joint positions.

4. Stuff the limbs and close the openings.

5. Stuff the body and close the opening. Don't forget to insert your identification tag if you have one (see page 18).

INSTRUCTIONS - TRIMMING

1. Clip the muzzle fur if desired (see page 14).

2. Finish your bear with a decorative bow or dress with clothes of your choice from Chapter 5, groom with a wire brush and ease any trapped fur away from the seams.

Plate 1 Scallywag – Illustrating the variety achievable from the basic pattern.
Clockwise from the top left—Large Scallytwag, Scallywag, young Scallywag (all using short muzzle version of the basic pattern) Young Scallyag with long muzzle.

Plate 2 Clockwise from top –Thread - stranded cotton, perle 8 or 5; Eyes - German glass, snaplock; Plastic beads for filling; Ginned cotton wadding; Lead shot pellets; instant setting glue for head joint bolts; Pliers and joints - plastic, cotter pin, locknut; Plastic beads for filling; Polyfill wadding and cotterpin turner; Strong thread - Gütermann top stitch and forceps.

Plate 3 Jewellery pillow - Sculptured applique is the centrepiece of this beautiful display pillow.

Plate 4 Mini bears for special occasions Valentine, Jester, flower fairy.
Mini bears - fun in the garden.

LARGE SCALLYWAG

36 cm (14"); 24 cm (9 ½") when sitting
Colour plate 1

FABRICS

Fabrics with a pile length of 1.6 cm (⅝") to 1.9 cm (¾") will give good results for this pattern size. German swirly mohair with a 1.6 cm (⅝") length pile was used for the bear pictured at the top of the cover picture and also in the colour pages. **Enlarge pattern pieces on a photocopier to 130% of the original size.**

MATERIALS

- *Mohair, 50 cm x 46.5 cm (20" x 18 ¼")*
- *1 set of joints with 30 mm (1 ¼") discs for the head and 25 mm (1") discs for the limbs*
- *1 pair of 8 or 9 mm glass eyes*
- *Felt or suede, 11 cm x 14 cm (4 ¼" x 5 ½"), for the paws*
- *Coton Perle 5 or 8 for the nose and mouth*
- *Strong thread for sewing*
- *Stuffing of your choice*

INSTRUCTIONS

1. Enlarge pattern pieces on a photocopier to 130% of the original size.

2. Then follow the instructions given on page 20 for the 25 cm (10") Scallywag.

YOUNG SCALLYWAG

17-18 cm (7"); 12-13 cm (5") when sitting
Colour plate 1

FABRICS

This little bear has enormous character when made with the bent leg version of the pattern and the shorter muzzle. Weighted pellet filling and slightly looser joints will make him very poseable.

You can use a variety of fabrics: German woven back rayon (see the bear in the middle of the centre row of the cover picture and in the colour pages) which is not as easy to handle as mohair; German mohair, 7 mm (5⁄16") pile, used for the bear in the top drawer on the far right of the cover picture; or German mohair, sparse 7 mm (5⁄16") as used for the bear in the lower right of the cover picture and also in the colour pages. **Reduce pattern pieces on photocopier to 70% of original size.**

MATERIALS

- *Mohair, 25 cm (10") square*
- *1 set of joints with 15 mm (5⁄8") discs*
- *1 pair of 6 mm eyes*
- *7 cm (2 ¾") square of felt for the paws*
- *Coton Perle 8 or stranded cotton for the nose and mouth*
- *Strong thread for sewing*
- *Stuffing - polyester filling and lead (see page 14) or plastic pellets*

INSTRUCTIONS

1. Reduce pattern pieces on a photocopier to 70% of the original size.

2. Then follow the instructions given on page 20 for the 25 cm (10") Scallywag up to the stuffing of the limbs and body.

3. Limbs - stuff the hands, feet and around the joints firmly using fibre fill. Mix pellets and polyester filling to complete stuffing.

4. Body - stuff around the joints with polyester filling, then use pellets with a small quantity of polyester filling for the rest of the body.

Note: To make the closure of the seams easier, ensure that the pellets are well covered with polyester filling at the openings.

CHAPTER 3

TINY
A 14 cm (5 ½") bear with moveable arms and
legs jointed with beads
COLOUR PLATE 8

This pattern is designed to be simple to construct and joint for those who are inexperienced in bear making, and is particularly suitable for small bears. The tiny bears in the colour pages are made in mohair with a 5mm (*1/4"*) pile.

MATERIALS

- *1 piece of short pile mohair, 25 cm x 16.5 cm (10" x 6 ½")*
- *Four 5 mm (¼") round wooden beads*
- *1 pair of 4 or 5 mm glass eyes*
- *Stranded cotton for the nose*
- *Strong thread for sewing*
- *Polyester filling for stuffing*

INSTRUCTIONS - PATTERN

Refer to Chapter 1 for detailed construction methods. Note that all seam allowances are 3.5 mm (approx. ³⁄₁₆").

1. Make pattern templates (see page 17).

2. Draw the outline of the pattern pieces onto the fabric as shown in the pattern layout. Use a fine line marking pen to give a fine clear line for cutting.

3. Cut out the pattern pieces carefully.

INSTRUCTIONS - LEGS

1. Trim away the fur from the straight edge seam allowance B-B at the base of each leg.

2. Turn in along the seam line and tack in place.

3. With right sides together, fold the leg in half, and sew seams A-B.

Tiny

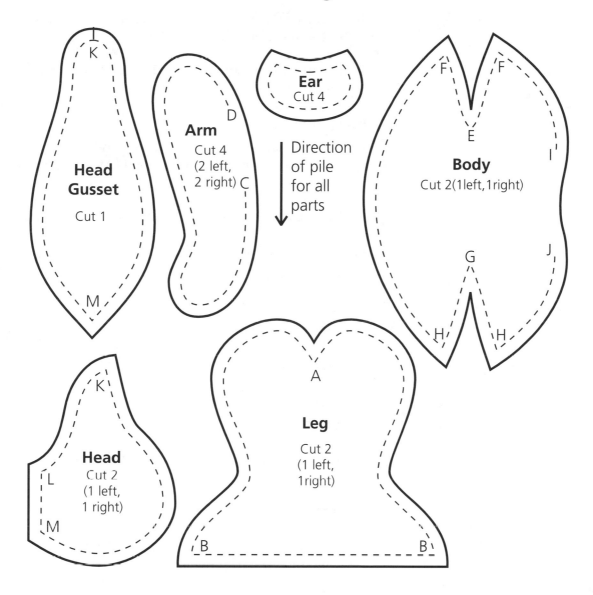

Head Gusset

Cut 1

K

I

M

Arm

Cut 4
(2 left,
2 right)

D

C

Ear

Cut 4

Direction
of pile
for all
parts

Body

Cut 2(1left,1right)

F   F

E

I

G   J

H   H

Head

Cut 2
(1 left,
1 right)

K

L

M

Leg

Cut 2
(1 left,
1right)

A

B   B

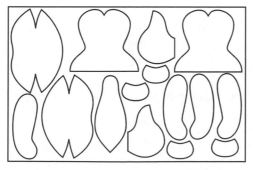

Layout for cutting
(1/4 full size) 25cm x 16.5cm

29

4. Turn, stuff firmly and close the seam along the base of the foot with ladder stitching.

5. The fur may be trimmed away to create a foot pad if desired.

INSTRUCTIONS - ARMS

1. Place the arm pieces right sides together and sew the seams, leaving open between C and D for turning and stuffing.

2. Turn right side out, stuff firmly and close the opening.

INSTRUCTIONS - BODY

1. Sew darts E-F and G-H.

2. Sew the two sections together, leaving an opening between I and J for turning.

3. Turn, stuff firmly and close the centre back seam.

INSTRUCTIONS - HEAD

1. Sew the centre front seam K-L.

2. Insert the head gusset, matching K and M, and sew the seams.

3. Turn the head and stuff firmly.

4. Run a gathering thread around the neck edge seam line, pull up and fasten off tightly.

Note: This thread can be left hanging to be used later to sew on the head.

INSTRUCTIONS - FEATURES

1. Sew the ears in pairs and turn right side out.

2. Position the eyes close to the seam line of the head gusset at the point where the muzzle ends and the curve of the face starts. Sew on the eyes with strong thread .

3. Embroider the nose and mouth (see page 16).

4. Sew on the ears.

5. Attach the arms and legs using the string method (see page 13).

6. Ladder stitch the head in place.

7. Finish Tiny with a ribbon bow around the neck.

Chapter 4

MIDGET

A miniature 9 cm (3 ½") teddy; 6.5 cm (2 ½") when sitting

Colour plate 4

Many people are hesitant about making very small bears but they really are not as difficult as some imagine. However, it is imperative that the correct choice of materials is made, most importantly, with the fabric. Most bear supply traders carry a good selection of fabrics ideal for miniature bear making. These fabrics are synthetic with a firm smooth backing which does not stretch or fray at the edges. The plush surface of the fabric has a smooth velvety feel and it is not too thick as this would make stitching difficult.

Many bear makers joint these tiny bears with fibre discs or metal washers and fine cotter pins. Midget is constructed with one cotter pin neck joint. The arms and legs are moveable and are sewn on after completion using the string method.

Materials

- *Fabric, 16 cm x 12.5 cm (6 ¼" x 5"), in a colour of your choice*
- *Head joint - two 12 mm (½") fibre discs or metal washers, three 6 mm (¼") metal washers and one small cotter pin*
- *2 mm (¹⁄₁₆") black beads for eyes*
- *Stranded cotton for nose and mouth embroidery*
- *Strong fine thread for stitching*
- *Small quantity of polyester filling*
- *Strong thread or dental floss for sewing on limbs*
- *Fine-pointed sharp scissors*

Instructions

Refer to Chapter 1 for detailed construction methods.

1. Using the pattern templates, mark out the bear parts on the back of the fabric as detailed in the pattern layout.

2. Cut out the pattern pieces very carefully; accuracy is important.

3. Match the arm pieces, right sides together, oversew and then backstitch.

4. Turn right sides out, stuff firmly and then close the opening with tiny ladder stitches.

Midget

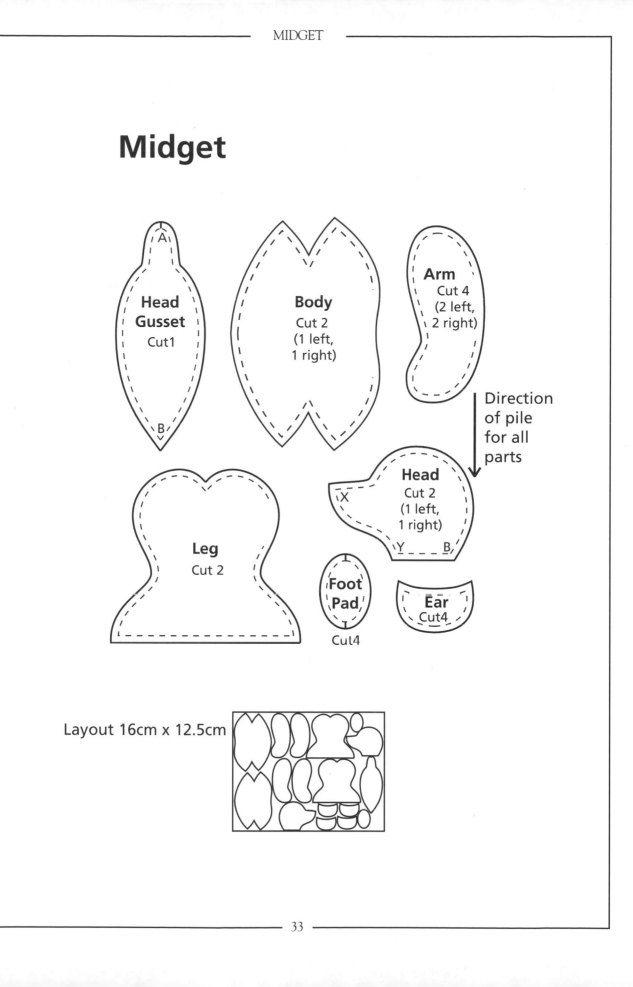

Head Gusset
Cut1

Body
Cut 2
(1 left,
1 right)

Arm
Cut 4
(2 left,
2 right)

Direction
of pile
for all
parts

Leg
Cut 2

Head
Cut 2
(1 left,
1 right)

Foot Pad
Cut4

Ear
Cut4

Layout 16cm x 12.5cm

5. Fold the legs right sides together, sew as for the arms, insert foot pads the same way and then turn, stuff and close the opening in the leg front with ladder stitches.

6. Stitch darts in each body piece, then sew the body pieces together, breaking stitching at the top dart for the head pin. Turn through the back opening.

7. Place the side head pieces right sides together and join seam X-Y.

8. Match centre front gusset A to point X and stitch carefully in place. Work from point A-B on each side of the gusset when oversewing. Backstitching can be worked from B through A to B.

9. Run a strong gathering thread around the neck edge.

10. Turn the head right side out, stuff solidly, insert joint, pull up gathering thread and tie off firmly.

11. Match ear pieces together, sew and turn right sides out. Turn under seam allowance along the base of each ear and ladder stitch the two edges together. Carefully position ears with pins, then ladder stitch in place.

12. Attach the eyes (see page 18).

13. Work the nose and mouth using two strands of stranded cotton (see page 16).

14. Joint head to body (see page 12).

15. Stuff the body firmly and close the back opening.

16. Attach the arms and legs using the string method (see page 13).

Mini bears look very cute with a few tiny props or accessories. Shops specialising in miniatures are the best source of ideas. You can buy items such as miniature fruit, vegetables, hats, flower pots, baskets, garden tools and so on, but it is also quite easy to make some simple accessories. Our bears have been photographed wearing a range of outfits or accompanied by various props, instructions for which are given below.

JESTER BEARS

MATERIALS

- 50 cm (20") of 12 mm (½") wide organza ribbon (with a gold edge)
- 25 cm (10") of 2 mm (¹⁄₁₆") wide silk ribbon
- Tooth pick
- Beads or charms for decoration

INSTRUCTIONS

1. Gather along one edge of the organza ribbon to form a ruffle and tie around the bear's neck.

2. To make the jester's wand, wrap the cocktail stick with the 2 mm (¹⁄₁₆") silk ribbon and secure with glue at each end. Push a bead over the glue on one end. Sew tiny hearts or stars to the top half. The wand is then sewn to the bear's hand.

VALENTINE BEAR

MATERIALS

- Small piece of red mini bear fabric
- Small amount of stuffing
- Embroidery threads (Coton Perle 12 or stranded cotton)
- 2 mm (¹⁄₁₆") silk ribbon
- 3 tiny heart charms

INSTRUCTIONS

1. To make a tiny heart pillow, cut out two heart shapes in the red fabric. With right sides together, stitch as for bears.

Clip into the curves and trim the seam allowance across the bottom point. Turn through and stuff firmly.

2. Using Coton Perle 12 or two strands of stranded cotton, embroider bullion or detached buttonhole stitch roses (see page 87). Finish with leaves in 2 mm (⅟₁₆") silk ribbon. To bury thread ends, start and finish at the back of the pillow, leaving a tail hanging, and secure with a small back stitch on the front of the work. When embroidery is complete, pull the ends gently and trim against the surface.

3. To decorate the bear, sew a heart charm to one ear. Trim the neck with a silk ribbon bow and two heart charms.

FLOWER FAIRY BEAR

MATERIALS

- *2 or 3 fabric flowers with petals about 2.5 cm (1") long*
- *Pronged metal jewellery finding for crown*
- *Tiny pearl beads*
- *Strong cotton thread*

INSTRUCTIONS

1. Take flowers apart. Cut five petals down in size and rejoin to form a crown. Sew to bear's head.

2. Open out the prongs of the jewellery finding to fit over the centre of the petals. Sew in place attaching a tiny pearl to the end of each prong.

3. Make a collar and skirt by rejoining petals with strong cotton thread and tie around the bear.

4. Cover the waistline with pearls.

BEAR WITH SCARF AND BEANIE

See page 44 for knitting instructions.

GARDENER BEAR

Our gardener bear is wearing a tiny straw hat, about 5 cm (2") in diameter, decorated with handmade daisies (see below), and carrying a watering can charm. Handmade daisies also fill the miniature garden tub at his side.

MATERIALS - HANDMADE DAISIES

- *Small piece of water soluble fabric*
- *Small embroidery hoop*
- *Stranded embroidery cotton in chosen colours*
- *Small beads for flower centres (I used Mill Hill Antique Glass Beads No. 03024)*
- *2 stems of very fine (No. 30) green cake decorating wire*
- *2 mm (¹⁄₁₆") wide silk ribbon*
- *Blu-Tack*

INSTRUCTIONS - HANDMADE DAISIES

1. Place water soluble fabric in a small embroidery hoop.

2. Using a single strand of embroidery thread, carefully embroider daisies in lazy daisy stitch on the fabric. Complete each flower before starting the next one, leaving tails of thread hanging at the back of the work and a space between each flower.

3. Work the petals in the order shown in the diagram.

4. Cut out each flower; do not cut too close to the stitching.

5. Holding the tails of thread, dip each flower into cold water to dissolve the fabric. Leave to dry on a china or glass surface. Trim ends close to the flower.

6. Sew flowers directly onto the hat, attaching beads for centres.

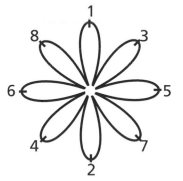

7. Cut stems for the daisies from the wire, turning one end of each piece into a very small tight loop.

8. Sew a daisy to the looped end of each stem, attaching a bead as the centre of each flower.

9. To make leaves, fold silk ribbon into small loops and wire securely.

10. Trim stems as required and arrange flowers and leaves in the tub using a small piece of Blu-Tack at the bottom to secure.

BABY BEAR

Colour plate 8

This bear has a bib and diaper made from tubular bandage. (Tubegauz Finger Bandage by Scholl was used.)

Materials - bib and diaper

- 12 cm (4 ¾") of 17 mm (⅝") wide tubular bandage
- 2 mm (¹⁄₁₆") silk ribbon
- Stranded cotton or Silk Stitch

Instructions - bib

1. Cut a piece of bandage 4 cm (1 ⅝") long, turn in the lower edge and slip stitch neatly.

2. Sew a length of 2 mm (¹⁄₁₆") silk ribbon (sufficient to allow for tying) across the top edge 2 cm (¾") from the bottom of the bib and trim away excess bandage close to the ribbon edge.

3. Using 1 strand of stranded cotton or Silk Stitch, embroider tiny bullion rosebuds, each made with 3 stitches of 8 wrap bullions, at the bottom corners.

4. Tie around baby bear's neck.

5. The wooden dummy is attached to the bib and a bow of 2 mm (¹⁄₁₆") silk ribbon is tied around the head.

INSTRUCTIONS - DIAPER

1. Cut 8 cm (3 ¼") of bandage.

2. Lay it flat and fold the ends in to meet at the centre line on the inside.

3. Stitch the top corners together on each side and decorate with bullion rosebuds.

4. Pull on to the bear.

CHAPTER 5

TEDDY TOGS

COLOUR PLATES 6 & 7

These knitted and crocheted clothes are simple to make and in many cases can be easily adapted to fit the individual bear you are dressing.

Scallywag's Jacket and coat

Following are the instructions for the blue jacket and the coat with matching beret worn by Scallywag in the colour pages. Tiny has also been photographed in the miniature version of this pattern. Coat pattern variations are given in [square brackets].

KNITTING PATTERN ABBREVIATIONS

R	row
K	knit
P	purl
st	stitch or stitches
St-st	stocking stitch
K1 P1	knit 1, purl 1
W fwd	wool forward
Dec or K2 tog	knit 2 together
Inc	increase by working into the same stitch twice.
WrN	wool round needle

MATERIALS

- 50 g (2 oz) ball of 8 ply knitting yarn (should make two jackets or a coat and a jacket)
- 1 pair of 3.00 mm (size 11) needles
- 2 small buttons for the jacket; 3 for the coat

INSTRUCTIONS

Note: Garter stitch (knit every row) except where stated.

- Cast on 30 st.
- **R1-R4:** K1 P1 rib.
- **R5-R18:** K.
- **R19-R22:** Inc 1 st at each end on these rows.
- **R23-R24:** Cast on 6 st [16 st for coat] at the start of these 2 rows.
- **R25-R40:** K.
- **R41:** K25 st [35 st], turn; the back is now worked on these stitches.
- **R42-R51:** K; leave these stitches on the needle or a stitch holder.
- At this point, the width across the back of the jacket can be measured on your bear. If additional width is needed,

add extra rows as required, then add half the number of these rows to each side of the two fronts.

Return to remaining 25 st [35 st] of R40 to work jacket fronts.

- **R1-R11:** K.
- Work buttonholes in the next row.
- **R12:** K2, W fwd, K2 tog, K6, W fwd, K2 tog [K6, W fwd, K2 tog], K to end of row.
- **R13-R14:** K.
- Cast off.

For the second front, work as follows

- Cast on 25 st [35 st].
- **R1-R13:** K.
- **R14:** K and continue across all stitches from R51, joining front to back panel.
- **R15-R30:** K.
- **R31-R32:** Cast off 6 st [16 st] at the start of each row.
- **R33-R36:** K2 tog at each end of each row - 30 st.
- **R37-R50:** K.
- **R51-R54:** K1 P1 rib.
- Cast off.
- Sew underarm seams, sew on buttons.
- Turn back top corners of the jacket fronts to form revers and tack in place.

Tiny's jacket

This jacket is worked from the same pattern using a single strand of Gumnut Yarns 2 ply embroidery wool and a pair of 1.25 mm steel knitting needles (see page 96). One skein is enough for a jacket.

Scallywag's beret

MATERIALS

- *Small quantity of 8 ply wool*
- *1 pair of 3.00 mm (size 11) needles*
- *1 flat button for decoration*

INSTRUCTIONS

Work in St-st (1 row plain, 1 row purl) unless otherwise stated.

- Cast on 60 st.
- **R1-R4:** K1, P1, rib.
- **R5-R6:** St-st.
- **R7:** (K1 inc in next st) to last 2 st.
- **R8-R14:** St-st.

TO SHAPE BERET

- **R15:** (K6, K2 tog) to end.
- **R16, 18, 20, 22, 24 and 26:** P.
- **R17:** (K5, K2 tog) to end.
- **R19:** (K4, K2 tog) to end.
- **R21:** (K3, K2 tog) to end.
- **R23:** (K2, K2 tog) to end.
- **R25:** (K1, K2 tog) to end.
- **R27:** K2 tog to end.
- Thread end of wool through the remaining stitches, pull up tight, fasten off, then use thread to join row ends together.
- Stitch decorative button to the centre of the beret.

Waistcoat for large Scallywag

MATERIALS

- *50 g (2 oz) ball of 8 ply wool*
- *1 pair of 3.00 mm (size 11) needles*
- *2 small buttons*

INSTRUCTIONS

The garment is knitted in one piece in K1, P1 rib.

- Cast on 46 st (for lower back edge).
- **R1-R14:** K1, P1.

To shape armholes

- **R15-R16:** Cast off 5 st at the start of each row.

- **R17-R18:** K2 tog at each end of each row (32 st).
- **R19-R42:** Rib.
- **R43:** Rib across 8 st, turn and continue working on these 8 st for the right front:
- **** R44-R67:** Rib. Inc 1 st at the neck edge on every alternate row until there are 20 st.**
- **R68:** Rib.
- ***** R69-R72:** Inc 1 st at the armhole edge on each row (24 st).
- **R73:** Cast on 6 st at the armhole edge and rib to end.***
- **R74-R86:** Rib.
- ****** R87:** Cast off 17 st at the start of the row (side edge).
- **R88-R92:** Dec 1 st at each end of the remaining st on each row (3 st).
- **R93:** K3 tog, fasten off.****

Return to remaining back st from R42

- Cast off 16 st.

Work front on remaining 8 st

- **R1-R24:** Work rows ** as detailed for the first front.
- **R25:** K1 P1, W fwd, K2 tog, rib to end of row (buttonhole row).
- **R26-R30:** Repeat from *** to *** as for the first front.
- **R31-R32:** Rib 10 rows.
- **R33:** Repeat buttonhole row.
- **R34-R35:** Rib.
- **R36-R42:** Repeat from **** to **** as for the first front.

White scarf for large Scallywag

MATERIALS

- *Small quantity of 3 ply baby wool*
- *1 pair of 3.00 mm (size 11) needles*
- *Fine crochet hook*

INSTRUCTIONS

- Cast on 16 st.

Work in garter lace stitch.
- **R1-R6:** K.
- **R7:** WrN, K2 tog to end.
- **R8:** WrN, P2 tog to end.
- Repeat R1 and R8 to achieve length required.
- Use a fine crochet hook to attach a fringe, made from short lengths of the wool, to each end of the scarf.

Scarf and hat for Midget
Colour plate 4

MATERIALS

- *1 skein of DMC Medici wool*
- *1 pair of 1.25 mm steel needles*
- *Fine crochet hook*

INSTRUCTIONS - SCARF
Work as for white scarf above.

INSTRUCTIONS - HAT

- Cast on 40 st.
- **R1-R5:** K1 P1 rib.
- **R6-R13:** St-st.
- **R14:** (K3, K2 tog) to end.
- **R15, 17 and 19:** P.
- **R16:** (K2, K2 tog) to end.
- **R18:** (K1, K2 tog) to end.
- **R20:** (K2 tog) to end.

- Pass thread through remaining stitches.
- Make a small pompon by winding wool around the first finger about 30 times. Tie firmly at the base and insert into the top of the hat. Pull up the stitches around the neck of the pompon and stitch firmly.
- Stitch row ends of hat together.

Dress, bonnet and knickers for Baby Jesse
Colour plate 7

CROCHET PATTERN ABBREVIATIONS

Ch	chain
Dc	double crochet
T	treble
HT	half treble
gr	group(s)
st	stitch
Sst	slip stitch

MATERIALS

- *3 ply baby wool (approximately 3 balls of 25 g - 1 oz each)*
- *2 buttons for the dress*
- *Ribbon for the bonnet*
- *Hat elastic for the knickers*
- *Crochet hook No. 14*

INSTRUCTIONS - DRESS

- Beginning at the neck edge of the yoke, make 69 Ch.
- **R1:** 1 Dc into 2nd Ch from hook, 1 Dc into each Ch, 2 Ch, turn.
- **R2:** 1 HT in 1st Dc, § miss 1 Dc, 2 HT in next Dc. Repeat from § to end of row, 2 Ch, turn.
- **R3:** § miss 1 HT, 2 HT in next HT. Repeat from § to end of row, 2 Ch, turn.
- **R4:** (increase row) miss 1 HT, 2 HT in next HT, § miss 1 HT, 3 HT in next HT. Repeat from § to last HT, miss last HT, 2 HT in turning Ch, 2 Ch, turn.
- **R5-R7:** As for R3.

- **R8:** Increase row - as for R4.
- **R9:** As for R3.
- **R10:** Work 10 HT gr as for R3, 13 Ch (for armhole), miss 20 HT gr, work 14 HT gr across front, 13 Ch, miss 20 HT gr, work 10 HT gr, 3 Ch, turn.

This completes the yoke. Continue on for the skirt as follows:
- **R1:** 4 T in 1st HT, § miss 1 HT, 1 Dc in next HT, 3 Ch, miss 1 HT, 5 T in next HT. Repeat from § to end of row, 3 Ch, turn.
- **R2:** 4 T in 1st T, § 1 Dc in last st of shell (i.e. st before the 3 Ch of R1), 3 Ch, 5 T in Dc. Repeat from § to last shell, 1 Dc in last st of shell, 3 Ch, turn.
- **R3-R18:** As for R2. Fasten off. (Skirt may be made longer or shorter as desired.)
- On wrong side, stitch skirt together at the centre back, leaving yoke opening sufficient to ease dress over the head.

To finish off, work as follows
- *Armhole edging*
  With wrong side facing, work a row of shells round each armhole: 5 T and 1 Dc in next st or next but 1 st, as desired.
- *Back yoke opening*
  With right side facing 1 Dc into opening with 6 Ch, as appropriate to form two loops for buttons.
- *Neck edging*
  Work a row of shells as for the armhole edging.
- Sew on buttons.

INSTRUCTIONS - BONNET

- Make 6 Ch, join with Sst to form a ring, 1 Ch. Do not turn.
- **R1:** 12 Dc into ring, Sst into Ch, 2 Ch.
- **R2:** 1 HT into 1st Dc, 1 Ch, § 2 HT into next Dc, 1 Ch. Repeat from § to end of row, join with Sst to 2nd of 2 Ch, 2 Ch. (13 HT gr).
- **R3:** As for R2. (13 HT gr).
- **R4:** As for R2 but 2 Ch instead of 1 Ch between HT gr. (13 gr).
- **R5:** as for R4. (13 gr).

- **R6:** (To double no. of gr) 1 HT into HT of R5 making 1 HT gr, 1 Ch, 2 HT into same st, 2 Ch, § into next gr work 2 HT, 1 Ch, 2 HT, 2 Ch. Repeat from § to end of row, join   with Sst, 2 Ch. (26 gr)..
- **R7:** 1 HT into 1st gr, 1 Ch, 2 HT into centre of next gr, 2 Ch, § 2 HT into centre of next gr, 1 Ch, 2 HT into centre of next gr, 2 Ch. Repeat from § to end of row, join with Sst , 2 Ch. (26 gr).
- **R8:** As for R7 but 2 Ch between each gr. (26 gr).
- **R9:** As for R8. (26 gr).
- **R10:** As for R6. (52 gr).
- **R11-R12:** As for R8. (52 gr). Fasten off.
- **R13:** Join into 7th HT gr from end of R12, 28 Ch (for ear hole), join into 15th gr from end of R12, 1 Dc into each st of previous row for 90 Dc (i.e. to 38th gr from end of R12), 28 Ch (for ear hole), join into 45th gr, 1 Ch, turn.
- **R14:** 1 Dc into 28 Ch, decrease across top by 1 Dc into next 2 st and skip 3rd (62 Dc), 1 Dc into 28 Dc, 1 Ch, turn.
- **R15:** 1 Dc into 28 Dc, decrease across top as in R14 (43Dc), 1 Dc into 28 Dc, 1 Ch, turn.
- **R16:** 1 Dc into 28 Dc, decrease as in previous rows (30 Dc), 1 Dc into 28 Dc, 1 Ch, turn.
- **R17:** 1 Dc into 28 Dc, decrease as in previous rows (22 Dc), 1 Dc into 28 Dc, 1 Ch, turn.
- **R18:** (To widen brim) 1 Dc into 28 Dc, 1 Dc into 26 Dc, turn.
- **R19:** Miss 1st Dc, 1 Dc into 27 Dc, turn.
- **R20:** Miss 1st Dc, 1 Dc into 30 Dc, turn.
- **R21:** Miss 1st Dc, 1 Dc into 34 Dc, turn.
- **R22:** Miss 1st Dc, 1 Dc into 33 Dc, turn.
- **R23:** Miss 1st Dc, 1 Dc into 33 Dc, 1 Dc in each Dc to end of row, turn.
- **R24:** 1 Dc in each Dc to end of row, do not turn, 7 Dc across base, decrease across bottom by 1 Dc into every 2nd Dc, 7 Dc across base, turn.
- **R25:** 1 Dc in each Dc to end of bottom, 3 Ch, turn.
- **R26:** Work row for ribbon insertion across bottom with 1 T into 2nd Dc, § 1 Ch, miss 1 Dc, 1 T in next Dc. Repeat from § to end of base, turn.

- **R27:** (Ensure wrong side is facing) work row of shells of 4 T and 1 Dc across bottom (10 shells) and around bonnet (20 shells). Fasten off.
- Edging for ear holes Work a row of 4 T shells and 1 Dc around each side as for bonnet edging (6 shells each side).
- Insert ribbon through R26.

INSTRUCTIONS - KNICKERS

- Begin front at waist, make 54 Ch, turn.
- **R1:** 1 Dc into 2nd Ch, 1 Dc in remaining Ch, 2 Ch, turn. Note: HT may be worked into the back of the stitches of the previous row to give a more interesting effect and to facilitate working of frills.
- **R2:** 1 HT in 1st Dc, § miss 1 Dc, 2 HT in next Dc. Repeat from § to end of row, 2 Ch, turn (27 HT gr including 1st HT and 2 Ch).
- **R3:** 1 HT in 1st HT, § 2 HT in next HT gr. Repeat from § to end of row, 2 Ch, turn (27 gr).
- **R4-R5:** As for R3 but omit 2 Ch at the end of R5.
- **R6:** Decrease by Sst into 1st 10 st, 2 Ch, miss 1 HT, 1 HT in next HT, § 2 HT in next gr. Repeat from § 14 times, 1 HT, 1 Dc in next gr, turn (17 gr including 1 HT / 1 Dc gr, leaving 5 gr of R5).
- **R7:** Sst 1st 8 st, miss 1 HT, 1 HT in next HT, § 2 HT in next gr. Repeat from § 7 times, 1 HT, 1 Dc in next gr, turn (9 gr).
- **R8:** Sst 1st 4 st, miss 1 HT, 1 HT in next HT, § 2 HT in next gr. Repeat from § twice, 1 HT, 1 Dc, in next gr, 2 Ch, turn (5 gr).
- **R9:** 1 HT in 1st HT, 2 HT in remaining gr, 2 Ch, turn (5 gr).
- **R10-R13:** As for R9.
- **R14-R25:** Increase by 1 HT gr and 1 Ch at each end to 29 gr at R25.

IF BEAR HAS A TAIL

- **R26:** Make hole by working 10 HT gr, 2 Ch, turn.
- **R27:** Make 10 HT gr, fasten off.

- **R28:** Miss 9 gr in centre, i.e. join wool in 20th gr from beginning of row, 2 Ch, 1 HT in 1st gr, 2 HT in remaining gr, 2 Ch, turn (10 gr).
- **R29-R30:** 1 HT in 1st HT, 2 HT in next gr, 2 Ch, turn.
- **R31:** Make 10 HT gr, 19 Ch, 10 HT gr, 2 Ch, turn.
- **R32:** Make 10 gr, 2 HT gr in every 2nd Ch, 10 HT gr in remaining gr, 2 Ch, turn (29 gr).
- **R33-R34:** Make 29 HT gr across the row. Fasten off.

IF BEAR HAS NO TAIL

- **R26-R34:** 29 HT gr.

FOR THE FRILLS ACROSS THE BACK

- With work facing so that wrong side of shells will show, work a row of 5 T, 1 Dc across the top row below hole, across 2 rows each side of hole and across 1 row at top, making 4 rows in all.

TO FINISH

- Sew up sides.
- With right side facing, work row of Dc around waist. Work 2nd row of Dc around waist over hat elastic. Before completing this row, draw in elastic to required length, stitch elastic ends together, then complete the row. Finish around waist, leg holes and tail hole with a row of crab stitch (see below).

CRAB STITCH

- With right side facing, work row of Dc in 'wrong' direction, i.e. from left to right for right-handers. Beginning with hook facing downwards, insert hook into next st on right, pull wool through, twisting hook to face upwards. With wool over hook, draw through to finish off 1 Dc as normal, insert in st to right for next Dc.

Smocked dress, bonnet and bikini pants set
Colour plate 7

MATERIALS

To fit	15-20 cm bear	25-30 cm bear
	(Waist 16-20 cm- 6 ¼-8", head 15-18 cm - 6-7")	(Waist 22-25 cm - 8 ¾-10", head 23-26 cm - 9-10 ¼")
	Note: Head measurement is taken from the left side of the neck to the right side of the neck, around the face and in front of the ears.	
Voile	40 cm x 80 cm (15 ¾" x 31 ½")	45 cm x 115 cm (17 ¾" x 45¼")
Narrow lace	4.5 metres (5 yds)	5.5 metres (6 yds)
3 mm (1/8") ribbon	1.25 metres (4 ft)	1.5 metres (5 ft)
Narrow elastic (pants)	To fit bears waist	To fit bears waist
2 mm (1/16") ribbon (pants)	20cm (8")	20cm (8")

INSTRUCTIONS - BISHOP STYLE DRESS

Size	Fabric		Measurements	
	Length	Width	X	Y
Small teddy	16 cm (6 ¼")	78 cm (30 ¾")	13 cm (5")	4.5 cm (1 ¾")
Large teddy	21 cm (8 ¼")	114 cm (45")	19cm (7 ½")	5.5cm (2 ¼")

1. Cut out the garment according to the pattern layout using the measurements from the above chart corresponding to the size required. Select the appropriate armhole pattern and trace onto the fabric at the top of the underarm cut-out panel. Cut out this shape.

2. Finish the top neck edge and armhole frill, marked A-A on the diagram, with lace.

3. Pleat the top edge with six half-space pleating threads.

4. Smock with the design below.

Smocking Design

Bonnet

Dress

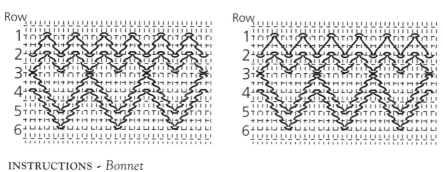

INSTRUCTIONS - *Bonnet*

- **R1-2:** 2 step wave.
- **R2-3:** 2 step wave.
- **R3-5:** 5 step wave.
- **R4-6:** 5 step wave.
- **R3 3½:** Work rosebuds in the centre of each heart.

Dress

- **R1-2:** Baby wave or chevron.Other rows as for bonnet.

Dress pattern cutting guide

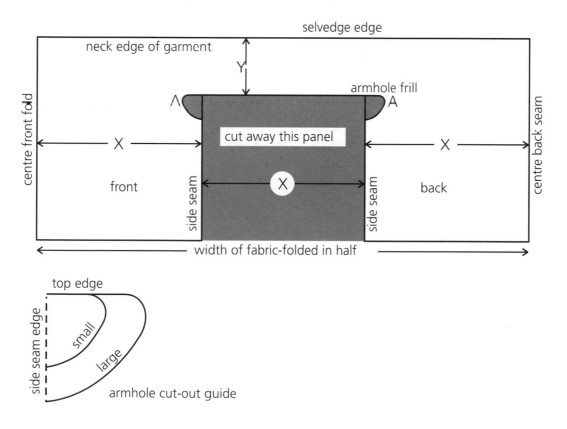

5. Remove pleating threads.

6. Allowing sufficient room to pass the dress over the bear's head, close the centre back using a flat seam.

7. Turn the remaining seam allowance back onto the smocking and stitch lightly in place.

8. Thread 3 mm (⅛") ribbon under the top row of smocking stitches, starting from the centre back and breaking at the front for the bow. Sew the ribbon in place at the back neck.

9. Stitch side seams.

10. Adjust length and hem as required. Trim with lace at the bottom and along the hem line stitching.

INSTRUCTIONS - BONNET

1. Cut out according to the pattern and finish edges with lace as detailed.

2. Pleat with six rows of half-space pleating and work the smocking design according to the chart, leaving four pleats unsmocked on each side.

3. Remove pleating threads. Check the bonnet for size by holding the smocked band around the bear's face and adjusting the length of the back panel so that it will hold the bonnet off the face when finished. If this panel is too long, the bonnet will sit too far forward on the face of the bear.

4. Hem both ends of the smocked section and the base of the back panel to form a casing.

5. Thread 3 mm (⅛") ribbon through one end of the front band, the back and the other side of the front band.

6. Fit the bonnet on the bear, adjust the ribbon to the correct length and secure at the front edges to prevent the ribbon from being pulled out.

Bonnet

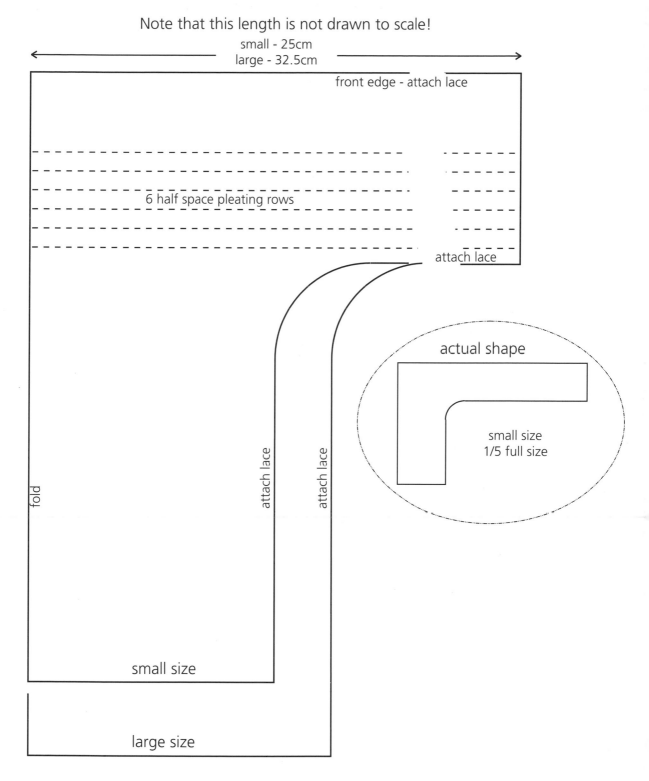

Note that this length is not drawn to scale!

small - 25cm
large - 32.5cm

front edge - attach lace

6 half space pleating rows

attach lace

fold

attach lace

attach lace

actual shape

small size
1/5 full size

small size

large size

INSTRUCTIONS - BIKINI PANTS

1. Cut out pants according to the pattern and finish the leg edges with lace.

2. Gather remaining lace and attach two rows across the back of the pants, turning in the ends on each side.

3. Turn under and stitch a narrow hem down each side edge.

4. Overlap the back side edges over the front section on both sides and tack in place.

5. Hem the top edge with a casing wide enough to thread with elastic.

6. Cut elastic to fit the bear's waist and thread through the casing.

7. Stitch on tiny decorative ribbon bows to hold the overlap section in place.

INSTRUCTIONS - SMALL RIBBON BOWS

1. As shown in the diagram, fold the 2 mm ($\frac{1}{16}$") silk ribbon onto a needle threaded with matching cotton.

2. Catch the centre with a stitch, then sew in place.

3. Cover the centre with two bullion stitches or use a needle threaded with ribbon to work a straight stitch over the centre of the bow.

Small Ribbon Bows

Pants

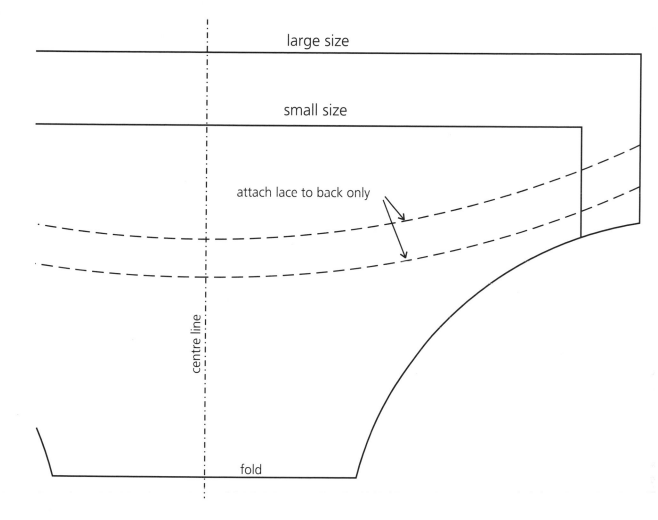

large size

small size

attach lace to back only

centre line

fold

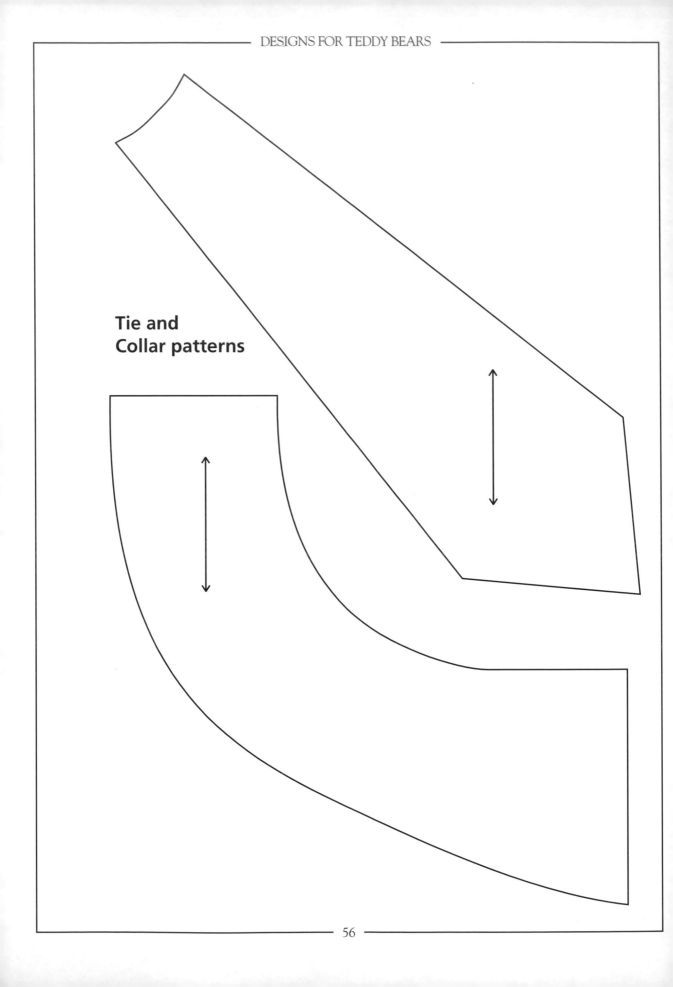

**Tie and
Collar patterns**

Waistcoat, collar and tie

Colour plate 6

This is suitable for a bear, 45-50 cm (17 ¾-20") tall, with a chest measurement of 40-42 cm (15 ¾-16 ½").

This outfit was made from a man's tie with a teddy design on it. Choose one with a design that can be well utilised. For example, a tie with even rows of bears on the diagonal, which permits sufficient room for a seam allowance, will provide the strips used for the strip quilted vest. With careful selection and cutting, two outfits can be made from one tie.

First, unpick the tie, remove the lining and press carefully.

MATERIALS - TIE

. *Lining fabric to compliment the tie fabric*

INSTRUCTIONS - TIE

1. Carefully mark out the tie pattern onto the tie fabric (it should fit on the narrow end).

2. Place the lining and the tie right sides together and sew on the marked lines, leaving the top edge open.

3. Cut out the tie 3 mm outside the stitching, turn and press carefully.

MATERIALS - COLLAR

. *30 cm (12") square homespun*
. *1 Velcro dot fastener*

INSTRUCTIONS - COLLAR

1. Cut a pattern template. Place on doubled fabric and mark around the outside edge with a fine marker or pencil (this will be the cutting line). Repeat for second collar piece.

2. Sew around the two collar pieces, 3 mm (⅛") inside the marked line, leaving the neck edges open (fig 1).

3. Cut out, trim across the corners, turn right side out and press carefully.

4. Zigzag neck edges together (fig 2).

5. Place the tie under the matched collar fronts and fold the collar and tie to the underside with a 5 mm (¼") turning. Top stitch through all thicknesses across the top of the tie (fig 3).

6. Turn under 1 cm (⅜") on the neck edge at the back of each collar piece and stitch (fig 3). This will roll the remainder of the neck edge under when fitted to the bear.

7. Check the fit on your bear. Ends should overlap at the back sufficiently to accept the Velcro dot fastener. Fold under any excess and attach Velcro dots to fasten (fig 4).

Collar and Tie

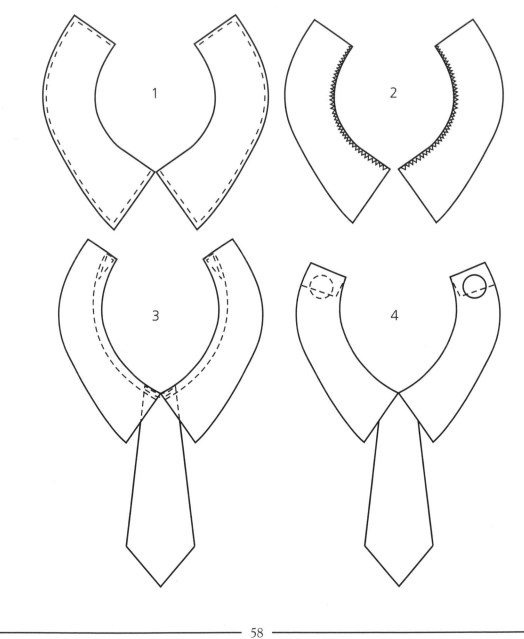

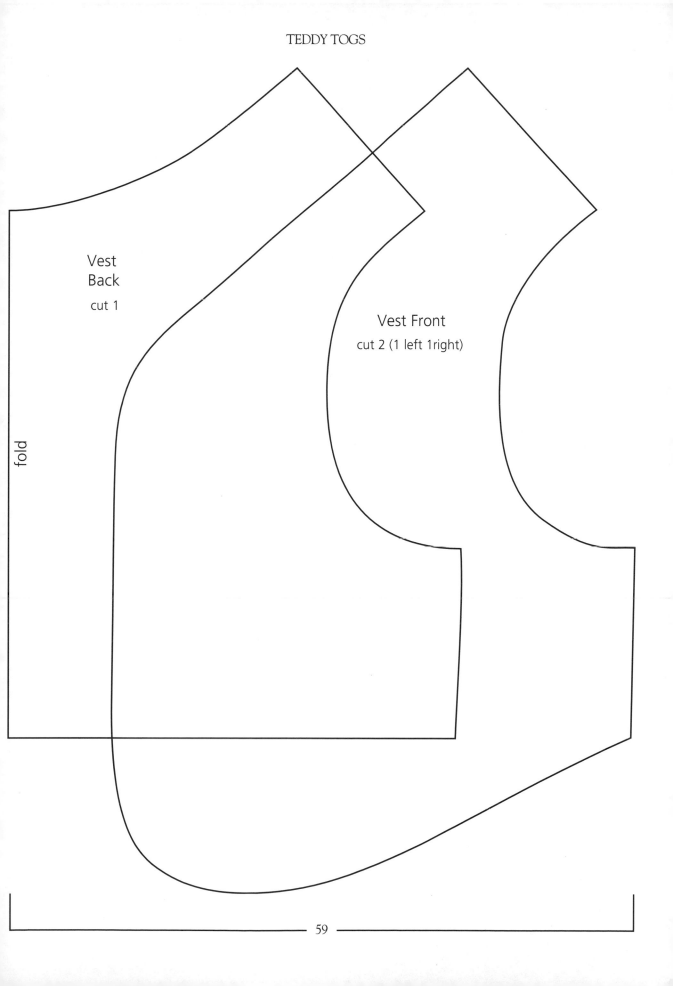

Vest
Back

cut 1

Vest Front

cut 2 (1 left 1right)

fold

MATERIALS - WAISTCOAT

- Fabrics to strip for strip quilted fronts
- Complimentary fabric for lining, back and bias binding (or purchased narrow bias binding can be substituted for this item)
- Calico for cutting pattern

INSTRUCTIONS - WAISTCOAT

1. Cut out pattern in calico, stitch shoulder and side seams, and check the fit on your bear for size. Make any necessary adjustments to improve the fit.

2. Cut two calico fronts using the calico pattern, allowing 1 cm (⅜") around all edges.

3. Position a strip of tie fabric along the neck edge of each front. Add a narrow strip of fabric along the lower edge, stitch and press towards the armhole edge.

4. Continue adding strips of fabric until the calico is covered.

5. Place the original front pattern pieces on the strip quilting and cut the fronts to the correct size. Cut two fronts from the lining fabric.

6. Cut two back pieces; one outer and one lining.

7. Join fronts to back sections, right sides together, at the shoulder and underarm seams.

8. Repeat for the lining.

9. Place the vest and the lining wrong sides together, matching the edges carefully.

10. Bind the armhole and outer edges with a narrow bias binding.

CHAPTER 6

APPLIQUE

COLOUR PLATES 3, 9, 10 AND 11

There are two different methods of applique used for the designs pictured in the colour pages.

Soft sculptured applique is used for the cushion and nappy bag pocket designs. This combines very well with hand embroidery and can be used on a variety of items including clothing.

Paint applique is relatively new. It was made possible through the development of suitable fabric paints. Based on similar principles to machine applique, it is quick, easy and practical. As Jean Townsend demonstrates in her examples, it can also be a real art form, yet it has many practical applications for clothing, cardboard and wood items, cushions, tablecloths, display boards, placemats, wall hangings, and so on.

SCULPTURED APPLIQUE

This form of applique is backed with fabric and does not always have to be stitched to the background fabric around all edges, producing a three-dimensional effect.

Simple backstitching can be added to lightly padded designs to emphasise features and any other important design lines.

When selecting fabrics, remember that the motif will consist of a double layer of fabric so be careful to choose lightweight fabric, particularly for smaller items. An alternative way of reducing bulk is to use a matching, lighter weight material for the backing fabric.

Stretch velour towelling is used for the bears worked on the pocket of the nappy bag pictured in the colour pages. The bear in the centre of the cushion (see Colour plate 3) is made from a plush upholstery fabric, but the velour used for the other bears would be equally suitable. Blanketing could be used for baby blanket designs but lightweight fabric should be used for the backing to reduce bulk.

MATERIALS - APPLIQUE BEARS

- *2 pieces of 12 cm (4 ¾") square of fabric for the small bear (bag pocket)*
- *2 pieces of 13 cm x 17 cm (5 x 6 ¾") fabric for the large bear (cushion)*

Note: Direction of the pile of the fabric should be from head to feet.

- *Matching thread for machine sewing*
- *Matching stranded cotton for hand sewing*
- *Small sharp scissors*
- *Small quantity of polyester filling*
- *Small black beads for the small bear's eyes; 3 or 4 mm brown glass eyes for the large bear.*

INSTRUCTIONS - APPLIQUE BEARS

1. Make a photocopy or tracing of the selected pattern. Note: If tracing the pattern, use white copy paper, not tracing paper. The pattern will be reversed as it is used on the back of the fabric.

2. Pin paper pattern to the reverse side of one piece of fabric.

3. Using matching thread and a small stitch setting on the machine, stitch through the paper and fabric along all the dotted line markings on the pattern.

4. Place the lining fabric over the stitched piece, right sides together, and carefully pin all layers.

5. Stitch around the outline of the motif (along all the solid line markings) using the same stitch setting.

6. Carefully tear away the paper pattern.

7. Cut out the bear, leaving a narrow turning outside the outline stitching. Clip into any tight corners or curves.

8. Cut a small slit in the centre of the backing fabric (the front panel has the machine-stitched design lines on it).

9. Turn the bear inside out and press carefully, making sure the seamed edges are pulled right out.

10. Pad the bear with a very small amount of polyester filling.

11. Pin the bear in place on your background fabric and slip stitch firmly along the outer seam line, leaving the ears free on the larger bear.

12. For both designs, outline the paw pads in back stitch,

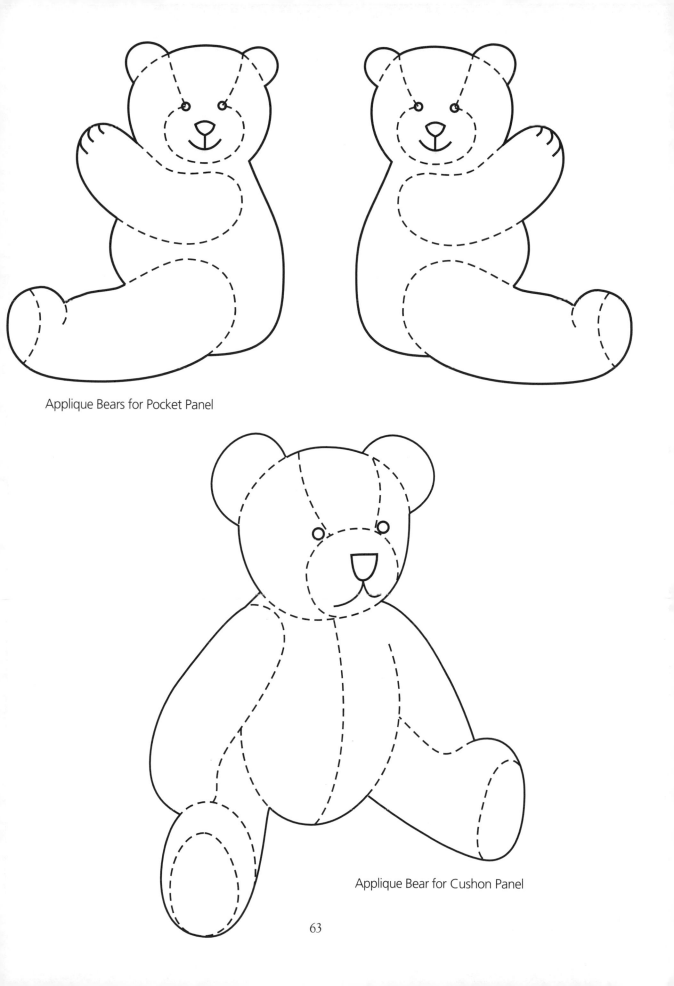

Applique Bears for Pocket Panel

Applique Bear for Cushon Panel

using two strands of stranded cotton, worked over the machine stitching lines - only on the surface, not through the padding. Work the centre seam line on the larger bear's tummy in the same way.

13. Work all the remaining marked sculpture lines in back stitch, using two strands of stranded cotton. Pass the needle to the back of the background fabric and pull the stitches firmly.

14. Sew on the eyes: black beads for the small bears; brown glass eyes for the larger bear. Use a stiletto or fine-pointed scissors to make a tiny hole to allow the shank of each eye to be pulled to the back of the work.

15. Embroider the nose and mouth with stranded cotton. (see instructions on page 16).

GUIDELINES FOR USING YOUR OWN PATTERN

Choose a very simple shape with not too much detail (for example, the brooch pattern on page 74 could be enlarged). Simple drawings are ideal. The large bear design was worked from a photograph of Midget (see colour pages) that was enlarged and then traced. Why not take a photograph of your own favourite teddy bear and create a design to applique onto a cushion, sweater or baby blanket?

Plate 5 Cross stitch designs for garments, pictures and cards

Plate 6 Teddy Togs for boys
From right to left - George models a waistcoat and tie made from a man's tie; Scallywag wears the coat (beret and scarf hang on the chair); Large Scallywag wears his waistcoat; Tiny models his miniature jacket.

Plate 7 Girls outfits include knitted jackets, crochet dress and bonnet and a pretty smocked outfit.

Plate 8 Tiny's tea party includes Mum, Dad, and baby mini bear.
This charming embroidery can be used for pictures, pillows, blankets or a box top.

Plate 9 Hand stitched or handknitted these tiny brooches will charm both young and old.
Nursery items - Practical gifts for the nursery: bib, burp pad and nappy bag.

Plate 10 Fabric applique can be easy for decorating boxes. Embroidery is highlighted with a collection of bear jewellery to create a beautiful display cushion.

Plate 11 Printed teddy bear fabrics are used by Jean Townsend to decorate clothing items and gifts.

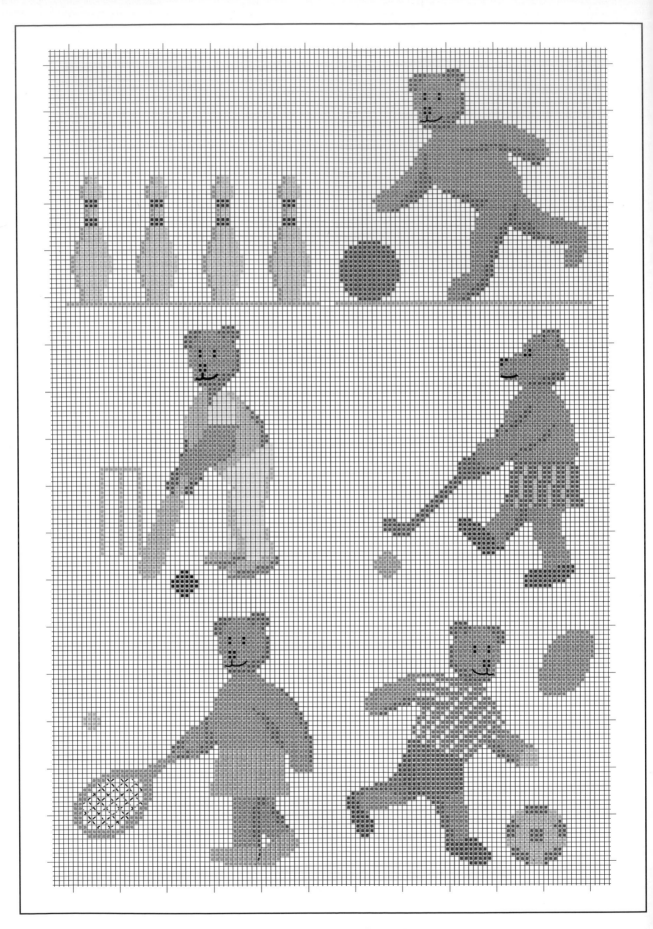

Plate 12 Cross stitch graphs

PAINT APPLIQUE

Designs by Jean Townsend
Colour plates 10 and 11

Jean Townsend is a talented fabric artist who has combined her passion for art, fabric and designing practical wearable clothing into a very successful business marketed under the label 'Originals by Jean Townsend'.

Use Jean's basic instructions to have fun decorating simple practical items, such as cards or calico gift bags, if you are hesitant about starting with clothing.

Jean has supplied the following information to get you started.

Manufacturers are constantly bringing new paints onto the market. The most suitable paint for applique edging is the glitter-glue paint which comes mostly in metallic colours: gold, silver, blue, black, red, hot pinks, purple and green.

The minute metallic fibres in the glitter-glue allow the glue to expand and contract more readily than with slick paints. The smooth colour paints are best used for embellishing, for example on beading work and fine drawing work, where paint is not put on in heavy or unbroken lines.

Paint manufacturers give very good directions on their products and it is wise to follow these to achieve a good result. Tulip and Polymark paints are excellent and reliable, but try any of the many brands available on the market to find those that best suit your needs.

Thoughtful use of these decorative paints will help prevent disasters, such as 'cracking', which can occur after washing. If you use your paints carefully, the clothing and other items you decorate will have a very long life and look attractive for years to come.

LAUNDERING

Wash garments inside out, on a gentle machine cycle, using cold water and normal washing detergent. Do not use eucalyptus oil based detergents as these will harm the glue base of the paints.

Dry garments naturally on the clothes line or clothes airer. Do tumble dry. Do not leave clothes lying wet for any length of time as this will damage the paint work.

Iron on the inside of the garment to help preserve the paint work and the fusible webbing used in applique.

MATERIALS

- *Cotton fabric, with print design of your choice*
- *Fusible webbing (e.g. Vliesofix)*
- *Garment or other item on which to place applique*
- *Glitter-glue paint*
- *Sharp scissors*
- *Iron*

INSTRUCTIONS

1. Iron the fusible webbing onto the back of the cotton fabric, making sure that the rough side (the web side) is against the material back. Use a dry iron as steam will cause moisture bubbles and lifting to occur. The iron setting should be determined by the fabric being used. Ironing time should be about one to two minutes.
2. Using sharp scissors, cut out your design, remove the paper backing and place on your project. Make sure that the position is correct before ironing the design on to the item; once ironed on, it is almost impossible to remove without making a mess. Once again, iron for one to two minutes, ensuring that all edges are well sealed.
3. Making sure that the paint is free flowing from the bottle or tube (old pieces of towelling are handy for this), angle the paint applicator at a 45° angle to the applique and proceed to apply paint to all the edges to seal the design. Do not be concerned if you stop and start. This is often an advantage! Any small bubbles which occur in the paint lines can be dispersed with a pin prick.
4. When applying the paint, use your imagination and add a few touches of your own to the applique, such as a leaf here, a swirl there, or furry ears for the teddy bears!
5. Use slick paints or puff paints to add pretty beads, bows, curls and ties, or flower stamens, to your design. These embellishments are what make the design your own.
6. Don't forget to sign your work! Achieving a high standard is really just a case of practise, practicse, and more practicse. You will be amazed at how quickly you become adept at controlling the paint flow and adding your own little touches.
7. Lie the finished work flat to dry. Drying time depends on the temperature and humidity. Generally clothing can be worn within four to five hours, however most things are best left for 24 hours before use.

CHAPTER 7

EMBROIDERY DESIGNS

These pretty embroidered pieces are designed to allow your creativity to shine through. Use them as a guide for your own creations.

Embroidered picture
COLOUR PLATE 8

MATERIALS

- *28 cm x 22 cm (11 x 8 ¾") homespun or similar (backed with soft sew Vilene if required)*
- *Stranded embroidery thread (single strand of DMC stranded cotton used throughout, except for the eyes) - Bear 677, 783, 781 and Black; Green 522 and 524; White; Yellow 726; Blue 809; Pink 224; Orange/Brown 720*
- *A Mill Hill crystal flower and petite gold bead*
- *2 small butterfly charms*
- *Fine line fabric marker for transferring the pattern*

Daisies

Bluebell

Clover

Tiny yellow daisies

Blue daisies

Grass seed

INSTRUCTIONS

1. Photocopy or trace the pattern.

2. Place the fabric over the pattern and trace the outline of the bear and any other areas of the design you require, such as the centres of individual flowers.

3. Do not mark the fabric with the exact position of all flowers and greenery as it is intended to be a free design offering an opportunity for your own creativity.

4. If you wish, back fabric with Soft Sew Vilene.

5. The bear is embroidered in long and short stitch (see page 93) using a single strand of thread to simulate fur. Care should be taken to work the stitching in the right direction. Mix colours 783 and 781 to fill in the main body parts. Work with 781 only where heavier shadow is required, for example, around the muzzle and along the gusset lines on the face, on the body below the arm, on the leg and ankle crease, and around the foot pad.

6. Work the muzzle in 677, radiating stitches out from the nose area. The inner ear and paw pads are worked in satin stitch, using the same thread. Use two strands of black to work a single colonial knot for each eye. Highlight the eyes with a tiny straight stitch in white. Embroider the nose and mouth with a single strand of thread.

7. Work the background greenery: two closely worked rows of stem stitch in 522 for the grasses and a single row of stem stitch in 524 for the stems of flowers.

8. Work flowers as follows (see pattern, page 67, and Chapter 12 for flower details):

    Daisies: Uneven lazy daisy in white for the petals; colonial knots in 726 for the centres.

    Clover: Lazy daisy in 224.

    Bluebells: Lazy daisy in 809.

    Tiny daisies: Lazy daisy in 726, with a single colonial knot in 720 for the centres.

    Blue daisies: Colonial knots in 809, with a single yellow knot in 726 for the centres.

9. Add some leaves in uneven lazy daisy stitch (see page 92) where appropriate. Work stem for the flower held by the bear.

10. Work grass seed heads in using a single palestrina stitch (see page 93).

11. Press embroidery carefully - face down on a towel is ideal-before attaching charms.

12. Attach crystal flower by threading the petite bread to sit in the centre of the flower.

Jewellery pillow
COLOUR PLATE 3

This pillow is 32 cm (12 ½") square, excluding the frill which is 6 cm (2 ¼") deep, and made from homespun fabric. The pillow illustrated was designed around a collection of jewellery pieces and teddy bear charms discovered over a period of time. If you have such a collection, you will need to take into consideration the size and shape of your own pieces when dividing up the areas on the pillow.

MATERIALS FOR A SIMILAR PILLOW

- *Fabric and a cushion insert for the chosen pillow size*
- *Lace, entredeux, ribbons and assorted threads for embroidering line stitches to create the mock crazy patchwork surrounding the centre panel*
- *Embroidery threads, beads, charms, etc. for the simple flower sprays scattered over the design.*

Details of the original stitching are given in the key to the diagram, however this piece is intended to inspire rather than be copied stitch for stitch.

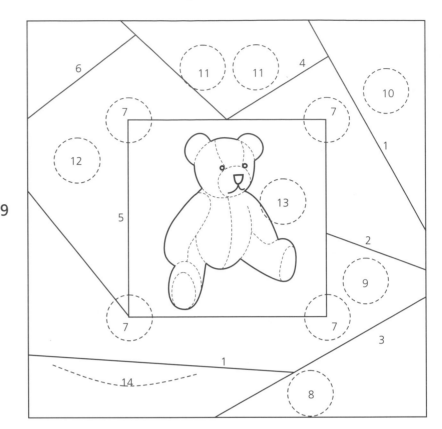

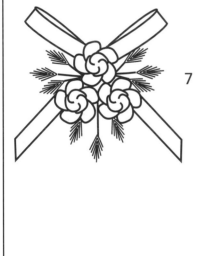

9

7

8

KEY TO PILLOW DESIGN

1 Guipure lace edging.
2 Broderie edging with twisted chain stitching.
3 Entredeux lace with ribbon insertion.
4 Palestrina stitch (p. 93).
5 Lace with ribbon insertion edged with palestrina stitch.
6 Single palestrina stitch buds covering a feather stitch background. Leaves in uneven lazy daisy (p. 93).
7 Detached buttonhole roses worked over a satin bow (p.87). Fly stitch leaves. Tiny gold hearts between roses.
8 Flowers as given for bluebells (page 88). Stems in stem stitch. Feather stitching with tiny gold beads. Leaves uneven lazy daisy stitch. Straight stitch bow.
9 Outline in green stem stitch. Detached buttonhole rose with pearl centre, uneven lazy daisy buds and leaves interspersed with tiny pearls (p. 92).
10 Flowers formed with five colonial knots and a tiny bead for the centre. Design finished with tightly packed green colonial knots (p. 88).

11 Daisies worked in uneven lazy daisy stitch (see page 92) with tiny bead centres. Stems in stem stitch. Leaves in uneven lazy daisy stitch.

12 Outline in green stem stitch. Bell-shaped flowers in gold worked with three lazy daisy stitches, and buds worked with two and one stitches. Leaves are in uneven lazy daisy stitch.

13 Stems in stem stitch. Flowers are daisies (see page 88) and detached buttonhole stitch roses with pearl centres (p. 87). Centre flower is a Mill Hill crystal flower. Leaves are uneven lazy daisy.

14 Feather stitch garland with three small pearl-centred roses in the middle (p. 87). Three-petal tulip- shaped flowers in uneven lazy daisy mixed with tiny beads and lazy daisy leaves.

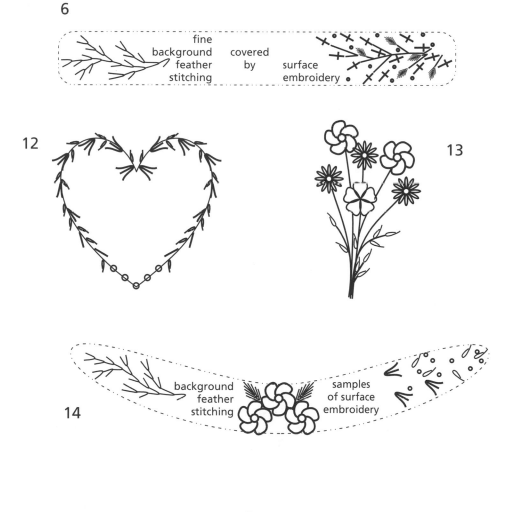

CHAPTER 8

TEDDY BEAR BROOCHES

Colour plate 9

Knitted bear brooch

MATERIALS

- *1 skein of Gumnut Yarns 2 ply embroidery wool (sufficient for 3 bears)*
- *1 pair of steel 1.25 mm lace knitting needles*
- *Small quantity of filling*
- *Embroidery thread for features*
- *2 Mill Hill beads No.00081 for eyes*
- *1 brooch back or small gold safety pin*

INSTRUCTIONS

See page 40 for abbreviations. Use a single strand of the wool.

- Cast on 6 st (head).
- **R1:** Inc into every stitch.
- **R2:** P.
- **R3:** K2, (Inc in next 2 st. K3) twice (16 st).
- **R4-R12:** St-st.

To shape neck:

- **R13:** K3, K2 tog, K2, K2 tog, K2, K2 tog, K3.
- **R14:** P.
- **R15:** K3, Inc, K2, Inc, K2, Inc, K3.
- **R16:** P.
- **R17:** K6, Inc, K2, Inc, K6.
- **R18-R22:** St-st.
- **R23:** K3, K2 tog, K8, K2 tog, K3.
- **R24:** P.
- **R25:** K7, Inc in next st. turn and continue working on these 9 st for the leg.
- **R26-R31:** St-st.

Thread wool through stitch and pull up firmly.

Return to remaining 8 st from R24.

R1: Inc in 1st st. K to end

R2-R7: St:st

R1-R7: St-st.

Finish as for first leg.

To knit arm:

Cast on 4 st.

R1: Inc into each st.

R2-R9: St-st starting with P row.

R10: P2 tog across row.

Thread ends of wool through remaining stitches, draw up tightly, fasten off and sew ends together from the right side. Stuff and sew closed at the top.

Repeat for second arm.

To finish:

1. Sew up body from the right side, working from the legs to the head. A chopstick or small screwdriver inserted inside the legs and body will make sewing easier. Stuff firmly as the back seams are sewn. Close the opening at the top of the head.

2. Run a gathering thread through the stitches at the neck shaping and pull up tightly, wrapping the thread around the neck again before fastening off very securely.

3. Work ears in detached buttonhole stitch using 10 wraps on the needle (see page 90).

4. Add shape to the face by using a strong needle to pull the stuffing forward to form a tiny muzzle.

5. Embroider the nose and mouth using a single strand of embroidery cotton or Perle 12. Work three or four tiny horizontal stitches outlined with a fly stitch for the nose and a fly stitch for the mouth.

6. Sew on bead eyes pulling them down firmly to emphasise the muzzle.

7. Stitch the arms in place.

8. Sew a tiny bow made from yarn to the bear's neck (see page 54).

9. Sew a small brooch back or safety pin to the back.

10. Reshape the muzzle if necessary.

Embroidered bear brooch

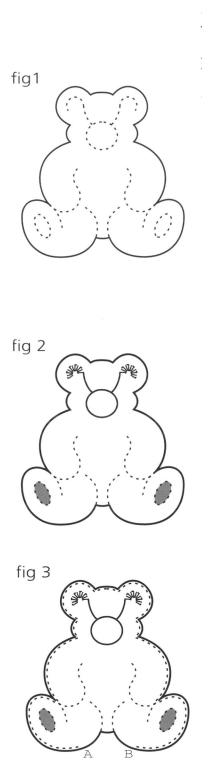

fig 1

fig 2

fig 3

A   B

MATERIALS

- *12 cm x 6 cm (4 ¾" x 2 ¼") of shadow suede, ultra suede or felt*
- *Stranded thread to match fabric, darker contrast to fabric and black for nose*
- *Fine crewel needle*
- *Small quantity of polyester filling*
- *2 petite Mill Hill beads (No. 40374) for eyes*
- *20 cm (8") of 2 mm (¹⁄₁₆") silk ribbon for neck bow*
- *1 brooch back or safety pin*

INSTRUCTIONS

1. Make a template of the bear pattern. On the wrong side of the fabric, draw the outline and markings shown in diag. 1. Working from the wrong side and using a single strand of contrasting thread, transfer the dotted line markings to the right side of the fabric with tiny running stitches (Fig 1).

2. On the right side of the fabric, using a single strand of contrasting thread and working just over the stitched outline, fill in the paw pads with satin stitches and the inner ear with buttonhole or satin stitch. Add tiny straight stitches to fill in the spaces between the running stitches on the face markings only (Fig 2).

3. Carefully cut out the embroidered teddy around the marked outline. Place this teddy on the remaining fabric, wrong sides together. Using matching thread and tiny running stitches, tack around the outline of the bear through both thicknesses. Leave open at the base, A-B, for stuffing (Fig 3). Note: The running stitches should be covered by the final whipped stitches.

4. Cut away the excess from the backing fabric, carefully following the outline of the embroidered bear. Using a

single strand of matching thread, whip stitch with tiny close stitches around the outer edges and stuff with care before closing the opening A-B.

fig 4

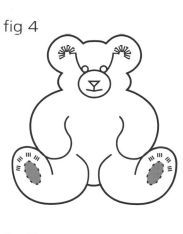

5. Using a single strand of contrasting thread, embroider tiny pads with two or three straight stitches. Add sculpture lines by stab stitching from the front to the back of the bear, placing the stitches between the original running stitches along the inner arm and the top of the leg. Carefully pull the stitches firmly to create indentation in the fabric (Fig 4).

6. Position beads for the eyes, pulling the stitches firmly to give form to the face. Embroider the nose in black straight stitches. Surround these stitches with a fly stitch and add a second fly stitch for the mouth (Fig 5).

fig 5

7. Finish with a tiny bow (see page 54), sewing the ribbon in place just below the muzzle stitching.

8. Sew on the brooch clip.

CHAPTER 9

CROSS-STITCH SPORTING BEARS

COLOUR PLATES 5 AND 12

These simple designs, featured in the colour pages, can be used for cards, pictures, hand towels or decorative panels. They can be worked over waste canvas and applied to garments or, as an alternative, they can be used in conjunction with knitting patterns to decorate knitwear.

The ten pin bowling motif was worked over 14 count waste canvas onto a purchased sweater suitable for a three-year-old. The design is 9 cm (3 ½") deep by 26 cm (10 ¼") long but the length can be adjusted by varying the space between the bowler and the pins.

The small motifs are each 8 cm (3 ¼") square when worked on 18 count Aida fabric.

Use one or two strands of stranded cotton, as preferred, on 18 count fabric and three strands on 14 count fabric.

Suggested colours are listed below.

CRICKET BEAR

Bear	Light Brown 842
	Mid Brown 840
Features	Black
Uniform	Bright Yellow 307
	Orange 972
	Pale Green 966
	Mid Green 989
Bat and wicket	Gold 783
Ball	Dark Red 326

SOCCER BEAR *(Rugby or Aussie Rules alternative)*

Bear	Light Brown 842
	Mid Brown 840
Features	Black
Uniform	Red 349
	Dark Red 498
	Blue 799
	Bright Yellow 307
Soccer ball	Dark Grey 413
	Ecru
Rugby ball	Light Brown 842

HOCKEY BEAR

Bear	Light Brown 842
	Mid Brown 840
Features and shoes	Black
Shorts or skirt	Dark Blue 312
	Orange 972
Stick	Green 368
Ball	Ecru or Black

TENNIS BEAR

Bear	Tan 435
	Dark Brown 433
Features and racquet strings	Black
Racquet frame	Green 368
Uniform	Green 369
	Orange 946
Ball	Green 472 or Orange 946

BOWLING BEAR

Bear	Light Brown 842
	Mid Brown 840
Features	Black
Ball	Red 347
Pins	Ecru
	Grey 762
	Red 347
Lane line	Tan-Orange 402

CHAPTER 10

NAPPY BAG OR SHOPPING BAG

COLOUR PLATES 9 AND 11

The bags illustrated in the colour pages are 40 cm (16") wide by 30 cm (12") deep, with side panels 20 cm (8") wide. A large pocket has been used to decorate one side of each bag. They can be securely closed with the heavy-duty open-ended zip.

Simple to make and comfortable to carry, the pattern can easily be adapted to other sizes.

The outer fabric used on the bags illustrated is homespun which has been quilted by machine (see page 82). Purchased quilted fabric or a stronger fabric, such as furnishing fabric, without quilting, can be substituted.

A contrasting print fabric was used for the lining. For the bags illustrated, teddy bear prints were used. The blue bag is lined with the same print fabric that Jean used for the paint applique (see colour pages).

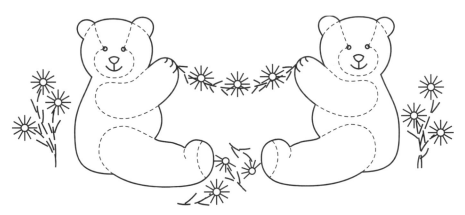

MATERIALS FOR ONE BAG

- *Outer fabric, 90 cm x 70 cm (35 ½" x 27 ½") wide, or 70 cm x 90 cm (27 ½" x 35 ½") wide for fabric with a one-way design*

- *Inner fabric, 90 cm x 70 cm (35 ½" x 27 ½") wide, or 70 cm x 90 cm (27 ½" x 35 ½") wide for fabric with a one-way design*

- *Pellon or soft sew Vilene, 90 cm x 70 cm (35 ½" x 27 ½"), if quilting is required*

Nappy Bag or Shopping Bag

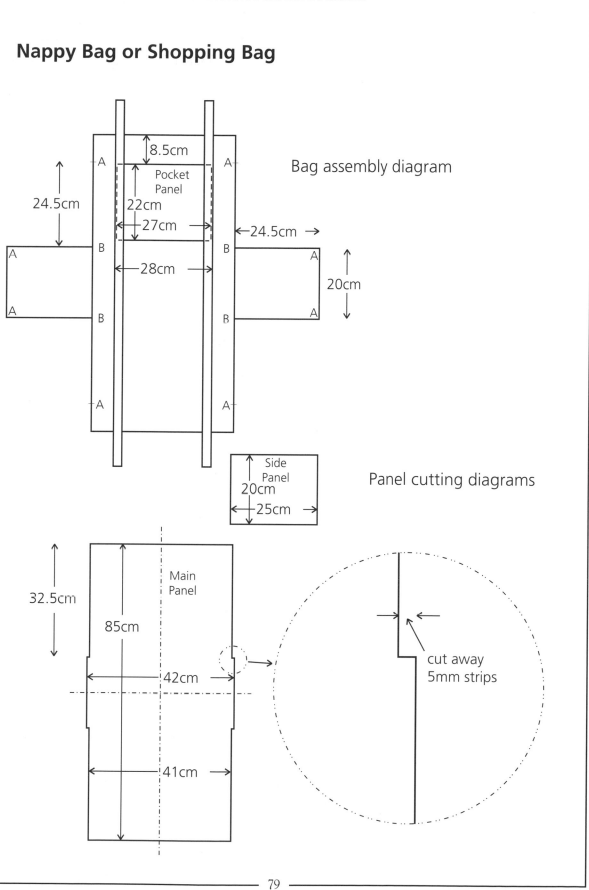

Bag assembly diagram

Panel cutting diagrams

cut away
5mm strips

- *Fabric for handles and binding, 20 cm x 112 cm (8" x 44"), or 2.5 m (2 ¾ yds) of 25 mm (1") wide webbing for handles and 1.75 m (2 yds) of straight binding for side seams*

- *Template plastic for stiffening the base of the bag, 16 cm x 36 cm (6 ¼" x 14 ¼")*

- *Medium weight iron-on Vilene, 19 cm x 40 cm (7 ½" x 15 ¾")*

- *Heavy-duty open-ended zip, 36cm (14")*

- *1 pair of wooden bag handles (these can be made from 62cm (24 ½") of half-round or D-shaped section, 20 mm x 10 mm (¾" x ⅜"), painted with stain and/or a urethane finish as desired). For suppliers see page 96.*

INSTRUCTIONS - BAG

Note: A 5 mm (¼") seam allowance has been included.

1. For each of the outer bag and the lining, cut the following pieces (see page 79):
- 1 panel, 85 cm (33 ½") deep x 42 cm (16 ½") wide
- 2 side panels, 25 cm (10") deep x 20 cm (8") wide
- 1 pocket, 22 cm (8 ¾") deep x 27 cm (10 ½") wide (decorate the outer panel as desired).

Note: If either fabric has a one-way design, cut two half panels for each large panel, allowing a seam allowance across the centre. Rejoin so that the pattern runs the correct way down each side of the bag.

2. Join the pocket panel and lining, right sides together, across the top and bottom. Press seams open and turn right sides out.

3. Centre the pocket 8.5 cm (3 ½") from the top edge of one side of the outer bag panel. Stitch across at 1 mm (approx. ¹⁄₁₆") and 5 mm (¼") from the lower edge.

4. Prepare handle strips (finished strips, 105 cm x 2.5 cm - 41 ½" x 1"). Cut or tear two strips of fabric, 105 cm x 6cm (41 ½" x 2 ¼") wide, fold in half and sew down the long edge. Press seam open, turn and press with the seam down the centre back.

5. Pin strips in place along the length of the panel, covering the sides of the pocket and having 28 cm (11") between the outer edges of each strip.

6. Stitch in place along both edges of each strip starting and finishing the stitching 8 cm (3 ¼") in from each end of the panel. Pin loose ends of strips to prevent them from being caught in subsequent stitching.

7. Stitch side panels to seam allowances on the centre panel of the outer and lining fabrics.

8. To stiffen the base of the bag, centre the template plastic in the middle of the wrong side of the outer panel. Cover with iron-on Vilene and iron in place.

9. Place lining on top of the outer bag, wrong sides together, matching them carefully.

10. Using a zipper foot and working with the lining uppermost, carefully stitch around the template plastic.

11. Centre the zip along one of the top outer edges, right sides together, and stitch in place using the width of the foot as a guide.

12. Repeat for the other side of the zip. (Zip will separate for easy sewing.)

13. Turn under the top edges of the lining and tack in place over the zip. Top stitch in place from the outside.

14. Bindings, 4.5 cm (1 ¾") wide, can be cut from straight strips of fabric.

WoodenHandle

Note that length is not shown to scale

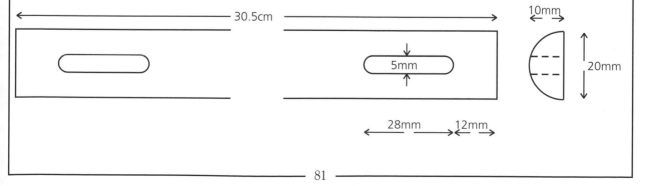

81

15. Bind the top edges of the side panels. Note that these panels should finish 8 cm (3 ¼") from the top edges of the centre panel.

16. Match the side panels, A, to the centre panel, A, on the outside of the bag and sew from A to B. Bind edges to finish.

17. Slip the handle straps through the slots in the wooden handles, adjusting the length so that they meet over the centre of the bag. Stitch firmly, trim excess if required, but allow ample length for the fold back as it is necessary to remove the handles to wash the bag.

INSTRUCTIONS - MACHINE QUILTING

A small attachment known as a quilting guide is available and comes with many brands of sewing machine. This guide makes the process very quick and easy.

An attractive variation to plain quilting is to use a twin needle and one of the fancy line stitches that many machines have. The use of machine embroidery thread will add an extra sheen to the stitching.

I always work on the diagonal, making the first row across the bottom right-hand corner.

Never tack the fabrics together as you need to smooth the top fabric as you go to prevent small wrinkles. If necessary, pin the fabric and remove the pins as you come to them. Bonding the fabric to the batting with Vliesofix fusible webbing makes the job even easier. Use a firm batting which will hold its shape and not catch on the feed teeth of the machine. Soft fluffy batting used for hand quilting is not suitable.

Always quilt a piece slightly larger than the size required and cut your pattern out afterwards. This will give a neat edge and any slight distortion that might occur in quilting will not be transferred to your project.

1. Cut a piece of fabric and a piece of batting.

2. Pin the pieces together, moving across the fabric from the bottom right-hand corner to the top left-hand corner, or bond with Vliesofix.

3. Set up the machine according to the manufacturer's instructions. Work a small test piece to check tension and spacing.

4. Stitch across the bottom right-hand corner, starting and finishing 2 to 2.5 cm (¾" to 1") from the corner.

5. Line up the stitched row with the bar on the quilting guide and stitch a second row.

6. Repeat across the fabric, removing the pins and smoothing the surface as you stitch.

Baby's Bib and Burp Pad

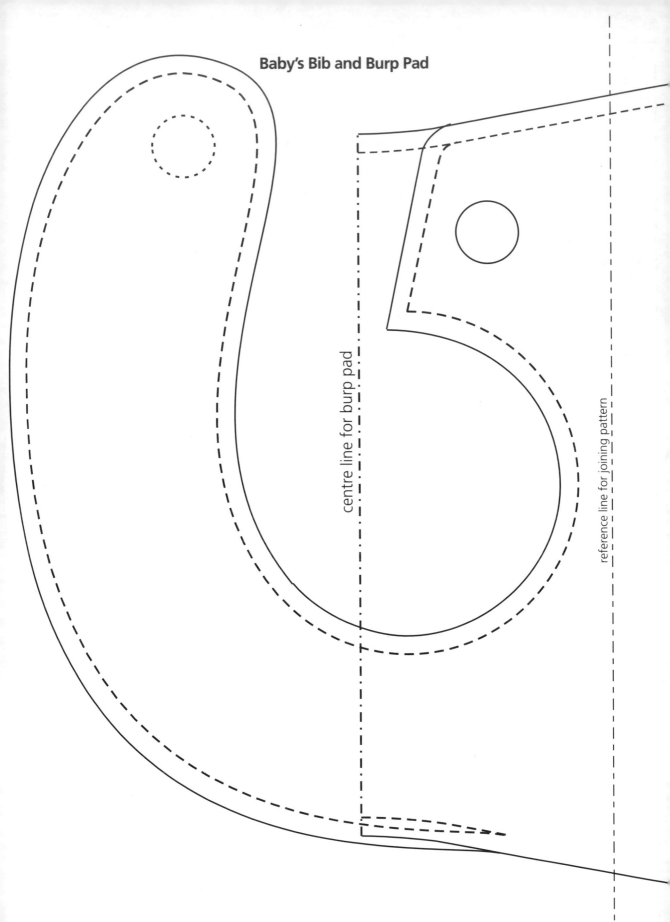

centre line for burp pad

reference line for joining pattern

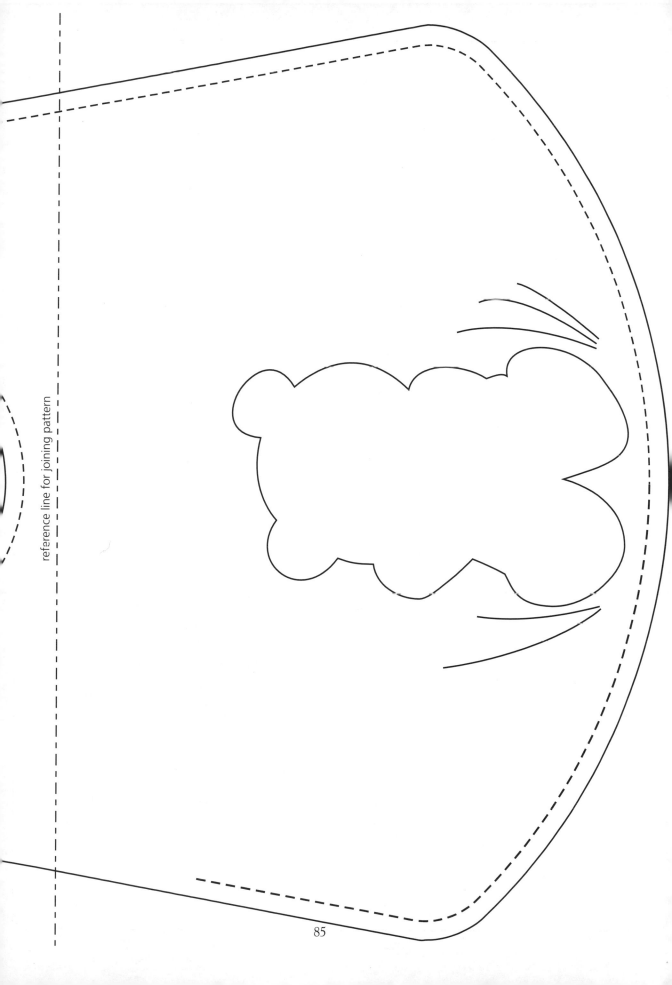

reference line for joining pattern

CHAPTER 11

BABY'S BIB AND BURP PAD

(to protect Mum!)
Colour plate 9

Iron-on teddy bear motifs have been used for this design. You could applique your own design or simply use a patterned fabric for the set.

MATERIALS - BIB AND PAD

- 30 cm x 90 cm (12" x 36") homespun or similar cotton
- 30 cm x 90 cm (12" x 36") flannelette or towelling for lining
- Vilene for tracing pattern (Vilene makes a good reuseable pattern)
- 2 motifs if required
- Iron
- Coton Perle 5 and stranded cotton for embroidery touches
- Velcro dot fasteners

INSTRUCTIONS - BIB AND PAD

1. Place the two fabrics right sides together. Pin the pattern in place and cut out.

2. Position the motif on the right side of the fabric. Iron in place and, for extra security, slip stitch around the edge with a matching thread, or sew by machine.

3. Work any embroidery highlights required. Press embroidery.

4. Place fabric and lining right sides together and sew around the seam line, leaving an opening for turning where indicated.

5. Clip curve around the neckline of the bib.

6. Turn right side out and press carefully, making sure that the seams are pulled right to the edge. Top stitch 2-3 mm (⅛") from the edge.

7. Sew Velcro dots to the bib as indicated.

CHAPTER 12

EMBROIDERED FLOWERS

Roses (Cast-on or detached buttonhole stitch)

These roses can be worked in a variety of threads, the type of thread chosen determining the size of the finished rose.

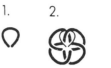

1. Using a straw or milliner's needle, work a ten wrap detached buttonhole stitch picking up two or three threads of the fabric for the base stitch (diag. 1).

2. Pull the base of the stitch close by stitching together with a tiny straight stitch before passing the needle to the back of the work between the anchor points.

3. Work four 12 wrap overlapping stitches around the centre stitch (diag. 2).

4. Change to a paler shade of thread and work a circle of six 12 wrap overlapping stitches around the outer edge of the first circle (diag. 3).

Daisies (Uneven lazy daisy stitch)

1. Mark the centre of the flower and work four 'marker' stitches at 12, 3, 6 and 9 o'clock positions.
2. Fill in the gaps with more stitches.
3. Fill the centres with colonial knots.

Clover (Regular lazy daisy stitch)

Start with a single stitch at the top of the cluster. Work rows of overlapping stitches moving down towards the base.

Blue bells (Lazy daisy stitch)

Work stitches down each side of the stem starting with a single stitch at the top.

Tiny yellow daisies (Lazy daisy stitch)

Work five tiny stitches around a single dot, then finish with a single colonial knot.

Blue daisies (Colonial knots)

Work a single colonial knot for the centre of each flower, then surround it with colonial knots, working as close to the centre knot as possible.

Grass seed heads (Palestrina stitch)

Work single palestrina knots along a fine stem, starting with one knot at the top of each stem.

BASIC STITCHES

COLONIAL KNOT OR CANDLEWICKING KNOT

Maintaining a flexible, relaxed wrist is the key to the successful execution of colonial knots. This allows easy change of direction as the thread is picked up on the needle.

1. Bring the needle up through the fabric and hold the thread between the thumb and the first finger of the left hand, leaving a loop about 8 cm (3") in length.

2. Slide the first finger of the right hand under this loop and sandwich the thread between this finger and the needle, which should be pointing away from you, and hook the needle under the thread (diag. 1).

3. Turn the needle anti-clockwise through 180° and hook the needle under the thread again (diag. 2).

4. Return the needle in a clockwise direction to its original position and pass the needle back through the fabric close to, but not through, the original exit hole (diag. 3).

To produce well-shaped even knots, always neaten the thread around the shaft of the needle, while the needle is held in a perpendicular position in the fabric, before completing the last step.

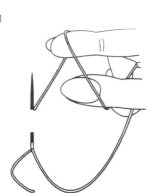

1

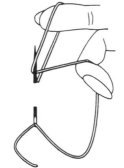

2

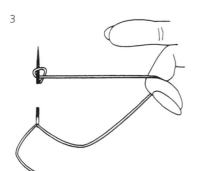

3

4

DETACHED BUTTONHOLE STITCH

Use a straw or milliner's needle to work this stitch.

1. Secure the thread with a small back stitch where it will be hidden under the flower centre, or a small knot may be used.

2. Bring the needle up through the fabric at point A.

3. Take a back stitch, going down at B and back out at A, taking care not to pierce the thread at point A or to pull the needle right through the fabric.

4. Slip the first finger of your right hand into the thread loop (diag. 1).

5. Hold the thread over the thumb nail and across the middle finger of the right hand to tension the thread as you twist the loop and slide it onto the needle (diag. 2).

6. Pull the thread until the loop tightens around the needle, making sure the loop slides to fit snugly at the point where the needle emerges through the fabric. (The knot created is a half hitch.) (diag 3)

7. Repeat until the required number of loops have been worked onto the needle, making sure that each one fits snugly beside the previous one. There should be no gaps and no overlapping loops.

8. Pull the needle through the fabric, gently holding the loops between the finger and thumb of the left hand. Tighten the thread until the loops fill the length of the core thread.

9. Anchor the stitch by passing the needle to the back of the work at point B. For loop stitches, used for petals, A and B are close together to form the stitch into a cup shape, as required for some flowers.

10. Pull the base of the stitch in closer by stitching together the first and last knot, as shown in diagrams 5, 6 and 7.

POINTS TO REMEMBER

1. The shape of the finished stitch will be governed by the length of the foundation back stitch and the number of loops worked onto the needle.

2. Tighten the core thread carefully so that the loops fill the thread sufficiently. Too few loops worked for the size of the stitch required will result in a loose floppy stitch that will not retain the shape of the flower.

3. Care must be taken not to pull the back stitch too tight as you lay the stitch or the base fabric will pucker. This is most likely to happen if there are too few loops worked onto the needle.

FEATHER STITCH

This stitch is useful for defining a shape that will be embroidered with a random selection of flowers. It can also be very useful as a background fill of fern-type leaves.

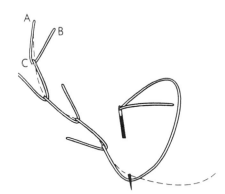

1. Bring the needle up at A at the top of the line to be followed.

2. Take the needle down through the fabric below this point and to the right of the line (point B).

3. Slant the needle down slightly and bring it back to the surface on the line with the thread looped under the needle. Pull the needle through (point C).

4. Repeat the stitch, inserting the needle to the left of the centre line. Continue working down the line, alternating the stitches from side to side.

5. This is a 'one-way' stitch. Take care that all the stems point in the right direction on a design.

FLY STITCH

1. Bring the needle up at A, then down at B and out again at C. Keep the thread from point A looped under the needle at C and pull the needle through (diag. 1).

2. Anchor the stitch by passing the needle to the back of the work at D (diag. 2). Note that a small stalk can be created by moving point D further away from point C.

LADDER STITCH

Use ladder stitch to close all seams after stuffing.
1. Fold the seam allowance to the inside along the stitching line.

2. Pick up a few threads of fabric along the seam line on one side, then pick up the same number of threads along the other side of the opening. The crossover thread represents a rung of the ladder and should be straight; the pick up sections represent the side supports. As long as strong thread is used, several stitches can be worked and then tightened really firmly to pull the two sides together securely.

LAZY DAISY STITCH

1. Bring the needle up at A, take it back down at A and out again at B, looping the thread under the point of the needle.

2. Pull the needle through the fabric, tightening the thread gently. Anchor with a small stitch at the point of the stitch.

UNEVEN LAZY DAISY

To work uneven lazy daisy, the stitch is turned around and is started at the pointed end of the flower or leaf and anchored at the centre or base. It is a useful stitch that can be used for leaves and buds.

1. Bring the needle up at A. take it down at B and out at C, passing the thread under the point from left to right of the needle.This gives a finer tip to the petals than is possible with ordinary lazy daisy stitch.

2. Adjust the distance between points A and B as required.

LONG AND SHORT SATIN STITCH

The first row of stitching is worked with alternating long and short stitches, the next and every following row is worked with stitches of about the same length so that the background fabric is completely covered. It is not necessary to start and finish the stitches using the same needle holes. To achieve a more natural fur effect, overlap the stitches and if desired, work some off-line stitches.

PALESTRINA OR DOUBLE KNOT STITCH

If possible, use a tapestry needle for this stitch to avoid splitting the working thread or picking up threads from the background fabric. If piercing the base fabric is too hard with a blunt needle, use a sharp needle but lead with the needle eye instead of the point when working under the stitches. Note that the needle must always pass from the top downwards when working over the bar stitch.

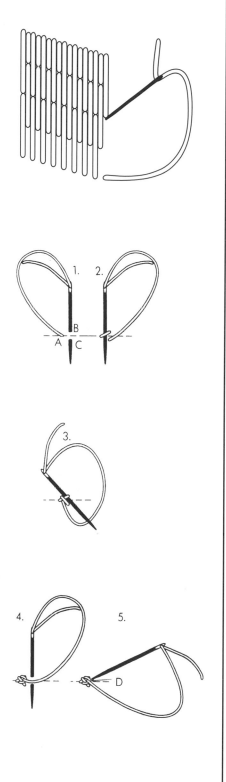

1. Working from left to right, come up at point A on the line to be covered, take a small vertical stitch entering the fabric above the design line at B and bring the needle up below the line at C (diag. 1). Pull the needle through and tighten the thread to form a small bar stitch. The distance between points B and C will depend on the thickness of the threads used and the texture required.

2. Keeping the thread to the right, slide the needle under the bar stitch from above and pull through (diag. 2).

3. Allowing the thread to form a loop below the stitch, pass the needle under the bar stitch a second time, working through the top corner of the bar above the stitch just completed. Pull it through, keeping the needle on top of the thread loop (diag. 4).

4. To work a line of these stitches, repeat the stitch as shown in diag. 4.

5. To work a single stitch for flower buds or sprays, work a single stitch, as described, starting at point A at the tip of the bud and finishing by passing the needle to the back of the work at point D (diag. 5).

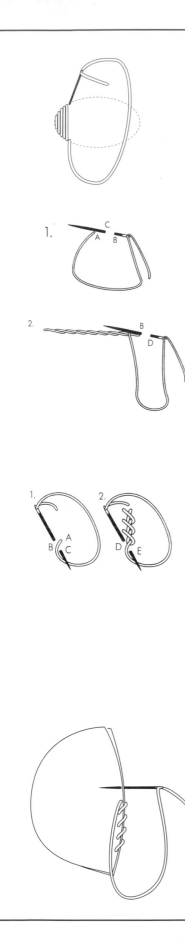

SATIN STITCH

Pass the needle up from the back of the work and lay stitches across the area being worked to cover the ground fabric. Keep the stitches close and even.

STEM OR OUTLINE STITCH

1. Bring the needle out at A, down at B and out again at C (where C is halfway between A and B) with the thread below the needle (diag. 1).

2. Keeping the thread below the needle, take the needle down at D and back out at B (B is halfway between C and D) (diag. 2).

Note that stem stitch may curve more smoothly if worked with the thread above the needle, depending on the direction of the curve. Whether you choose to work with the thread above or below the needle, it is important to keep it consistent in each line.

TWISTED CHAIN STITCH

1. Work from the top of the design down directly over the line to be covered.

2. Bring the needle up at A.

3. Form a small anti-clockwise loop of thread and pass the needle down at B and out again at C. Note that point B is level with and close to A but to the left of A, so that the threads cross over this point. The distance between A and C will vary according to the thickness of the thread being used. To maintain even stitching, the distances between A, B and C must be consistent with every stitch. When working a continuous line, be sure to keep the needle very close to the design line at points B and D (diag. 1 and 2).

WHIP STITCH

Small slanting stitches worked over two matching edges of fabric. The needle pierces both fabrics at right angles creating a sloping stitch as the needle is moved from one point to the next.

SUPPLIES

This is a rapidly expanding field and there are new sources of supply constantly opening up. Most suppliers attend events such as craft, doll and teddy bear shows and they will be listed in some of the many magazines now available on the subject.

All the suppliers listed below have been trading over a number of years. They have comprehensive catalogues and run extensive mail order services.

Dee Glossop Teddy Bears and Accessories
86 Model Farms Road
Winston Hills NSW 2153
Telephone/Fax: (02) 9686 1682

Gerry's Teddy and Craft Designs
30 John Street
Rosewood Qld 4340
Telephone/Fax: (074) 64 1479
Also at Bear World of Brisbane
Shop 18, Brisbane Arcade
Queen Street
Brisbane Qld 4000
Telephone/Fax: (073) 229 3644

Serendipity Collection
970 Mount Dandenong Tourist Road
Montrose Vic 3765
Telephone/Fax: (03) 9728 1979

OTHER SUPPLIES ARE AVAILABLE AS FOLLOWS

Item	Contact
Craft fur	**Pioneer Craft (wholesale only)** PO Box 373, Rydalmere NSW 2116 Telephone (02) 9684 4033 Fax (02) 9684 4333
Wooden handles for the shopping or nappy bag and books as referenced below. Steel knitting needles size 1.25 mm	**Jenny Bradford** 7 Noala Street, Aranda ACT 2614 Telephone/Fax (06) 251 1145
Paint applique; finished garments, fashion shows, demonstrations and teaching	**Jean Townsend** 77 Shakespeare Crescent, Fraser ACT 2614 Telephone (06) 258 4881
Hand-dyed knitting yarns and embroidery threads	**Julie Hanks** Gumnut Yarns PO Box 519, Mudgee NSW 2850 Telephone (063) 72 1886
Teddy bear stick pins and other costume jewellery	**RB Costume Jewellery** PO Box 321, Queanbeyan NSW 2620 Telephone (06) 299 1987

Other Sally Milner publications by Jenny Bradford

Silk Ribbon Embroidery for Gifts and Garments
Original Designs for Silk Ribbon Embroidery
Bullion Stitch Embroidery from Roses to Wildflowers
Textured Embroidery
Original Designs for Smocking
Jenny Bradford Embroidery Collection